ANY PATH
WILL
LEAD YOU
HOME

Embracing Life's Lessons
and Becoming Your
Exquisite Self

MARGARET M. DUFFY, MSW

Dedication

This book is dedicated to my daughters, Tacie and Maura. Having you both in my life has been such a treasure and has taught me so much about life and love. Having you has pulled all the pieces of life together in a way I could never have imagined and has helped create the beautiful tapestry of our family and our life together.

TABLE OF CONTENTS

Chapter Seven

Story 13 Death
Do I stay or do I go?

Story 14 Life
What Was, Is, Will Be

PART 3

Bringing It All Together

To sign up for a free ½ hr. Lightwork Session with Margaret or to listen to a free audio of this book please visit our website at:

Website: http://www.margaretduffy.net
Email: **margaret@margaretduffy.net**

INTRODUCTION - MY PATH

♦♦♦♦♦

Most of us grow up to find a specific path laid out for us to follow throughout our lives. Our parents raise us to follow a certain path just as their parents raised them to. Our teachers redefine that path as we learn and grow, and religions specify which way is good and which way is bad and set up guidelines for us to follow. There is the commonly followed path, some would say the path of least resistance, that is clearly marked throughout our lifetime and the expectation is that we will follow this path to happiness. If we're not happy, then it must be something we've done, it most certainly wasn't the *Paths* fault.

I don't know about you guys but what I was being taught, on some level, never completely set right with me. Path of least resistance? Holy crap, it couldn't feel more the opposite if it tried. My path brought pain not happiness or should I say the happiness was clouded over by the amount of pain on my path. And when the path made no sense at all to me, I was forced to formulate thoughts and ideas in my head, based on the rules and regulations on my road, thoughts and ideas that would somehow explain why the shit that was happening was happening, and guess what, I came out the loser in this venture. I took the blame because it seemed the only viable alternative.

I always thought about this process of life in a specific way as I grew up. It's like the highway and road system throughout the United States. There is the main freeway, heavily trafficked, with clear signs as to the right and wrong ways to go. There are on and off ramps that go to specific locations but it is the quickest, so to speak, way to get from point A to point B that I should follow. Most people travel it and never question what they might be missing along the way. There are major highways all across our country. They are on every map, you can see them from high up in the air and they are solid and well-traveled and always lead somewhere, and that *somewhere* is where I *should* want to go.

Even if I decided to leave this particular highway there were also clearly marked major thoroughfares that could help me maneuver through the city and get me to most major attractions. These roads led to places that were important to the majority of the population. I could stay on these roads and never venture to the outskirts and lead a genuinely good life. Or at least that is what the people spouting *least resistance* were saying. But who defined this "Good Life"?

On top of that there are side roads, back roads, alleys,

underpasses, overpasses, you name it, a multitude of different ways to get to any one destination. All of these various routes were manmade. They had been mapped out, plotted, planned   and contrived. The design of each was put into place to make it easier, more efficient, and more controlled for me to get around. But they were all made by someone with their own agenda and not necessarily with any of my unique needs in mind.

In life, I continuously met people who had an opinion of which route I should use. So many people have given me instructions, given me their map, but it never seemed to work for me to take their way. I saw the signs, heard everyone's opinions and then cursed the road because it often left me feeling broken down. Yes, it may have, at times, worked for a few miles, but truthfully it never felt quite right to me and eventually I wanted off that road.

So, say I wanted to take the road less traveled, so to speak. Say I wanted to find my own path, maybe even create a new way? Maybe I could get on my bike or in my four-wheel drive and go off-roading. Maybe I could go hiking to my destination. Maybe I could take an alternate route. Some of these paths may still have been manmade but they were mine and some were created as I journeyed onto them. All of them would have been my choice, not someone else's.

As ventured onto the alternatives to get to my destinations, they became increasingly more intricate, detailed and more alive. I could find ways where no one else had ventured. Some were rather rugged, others smooth and easy, but each one afforded me a shift in how I looked at life and therefore how I looked at myself.

I often imagined that I was up in a plane looking down at the world. At first I noticed the freeways shooting out across the landscape. As I hovered in the sky I also noticed a more intricate design. Roads weaving here and there. At closer inspection, I saw paths leading from those roads and noticed, maybe for the first time, that there were more ways to go then I had ever imagined. The system was endless, endless to creating my own unique way.

I must say I grew up with blinders on. I believed it was a very black and white world I existed in. That there was good, there was bad, and there wasn't a lot of in between. I was raised Catholic and there was definitely a doctrine that set up a way for me to live my life. It said that this was the way to live, we know, you follow. It wasn't even to be questioned because I was to take my cue directly from God. Even if you weren't raised Catholic, as I was, you can probably all relate to having strong beliefs cast upon you and a prescribed road laid out.

I grew up believing that there was a way, one way, to get where I wanted to go. Follow it and all would be fine. Stray from the path and perish. So, I stayed. I believed, I followed. I didn't question. I didn't wonder. I simply followed. I grew up knowing the major highways. I took them every day. But even as a kid, I wanted, needed, to go somewhere that was not on the map. In my life, a desire grew to take a more scenic route, my route where I could by-pass the path that made little or no sense to me and see the virgin country side of my own making. I just knew, deep inside me, I needed to do it differently from my parents, my neighbors, my friends and my church.

And then it happened. The shift, that deep-down I knew I wanted and needed but was desperately afraid to find or embrace. I was out jogging, training for a road race I was entered in and I was attacked and raped. I was nineteen years old and this tragic event shook me to my core. This one instance affected me in countless ways but what it did more than anything was to form a question that changed my life and my path forever. If EVERYTHING I had been taught was true, if the path I had been following was right, this wouldn't, couldn't have happened to me. And since it DID in fact happen, EVERYTHING I had ever learned, knew, followed, must be WRONG. A girl without a path at nineteen years old can be pretty devastating or completely liberating. For me it was some of both.

This book is about my journey. This book is about the likely and unlikely ways, paths, which brought me here today. When I began this journey, I was a highway driver. I only followed predestined maps and took only designated off ramps. I didn't question any of it. But the rape, this one event made me question everything. Now my life was one big question mark and my quest was toward the answer. And the answer was definitely off the path I had followed so far.

I have often heard people on TV or have read books where someone says that their way is the only way. I always cringe when I hear this. What I have discovered over the last thirty years is that there are as many ways home as there are people on this earth. I have learned that what works for one doesn't necessarily work for all and that each of us has a way and it is up to each of us to find it. We come with a built-in compass. We just haven't been taught or encouraged on how to find it and then on how to use it.

We each have our own unique true north. Our compasses are preset. As I am looking for and orienting to my compass, it is my hope that you too, the readers of this book, will also find and orient to yours. Our true north is our inner guidance. It will always guide us on our path leading us safely home. Our home is that place where we can truly be our whole selves and be the person who we have always been at our core.

This book is about that journey with my compass, finding my true north and what I discovered along the way. This book is a reflection of my deeper knowing that came to be, not because I hid from the deeper truth and meaning, but because I found ways to embrace the multiple facets of life presented to me. Every experience became a window into my soul so I used each experience as a catalyst for true change. I hope my stories are instructive for you following your own path and turning and embracing your true north.

CHAPTER ONE

STORY ONE – ALONE
Responsible For All

♦♦♦♦♦

I believe I have been here before. I didn't always believe that. I was raised Catholic and was taught of heaven and hell and purgatory. This was the one life I was given and on judgement day I would find out my fate. From the beginning I can't say in all honesty that worked well for me but that was where I started from. This was the highway I received instructions on. But along the way I couldn't help but look for other alternatives.

As an infant I remember coming into this life with one deep knowing and two distinct callings. My deep knowing was that I did not want to be alone this time around. I came in to a large family distinctly so that I would not be alone. My calling came from my belief that this family I came in with was my responsibility that I was here to make things right for them. I believed that it was up to me to make things better, and that I was responsible for their happiness. I also believed and knew, deep in my core, that I was here to finally love myself.

As you can imagine these callings, these two distinct ideas, didn't exactly go together. One led me to put my own needs aside and the other called me to turn toward myself in a way I had never seen nor imagined. So, my life became this dance. One part would lead and the other would rear its head when the pendulum swung too far either way. For me Catholicism must have relished my role as savior because I was selfless, giving, available and stoic. But as life unfolded I could not brush aside the intrinsic need I had for self-love, to turn toward myself, and this need grew, not out of this great love and companionship my path had created, but out of the deep loneliness that was there despite my family.

Alone is defined as being without anyone or anything, it is about not involving or including anyone or anything else and being and feeling separate from other people or things. Even amongst this great family I felt alone. Even amongst a neighborhood teeming with children. I couldn't explain it and it was beyond reason. I was surrounded by people, God was clearly in my life and yet something deep inside of me was missing and I felt incomplete and desperately alone.

This idea of heaven and hell and self-sacrifice started to unravel for me when life started to happen. I was basically a good person, tried to follow all the rules, was giving and kind, and offered prayer and loved with my whole heart. So, let's just say that despite all that I gave, shit happened. The truth of it is that lots of shit happened and what happened in my life could no longer be explained through the constraints of the path that I had come in on.

Bad things weren't supposed to happen to good people. If you lived life right everything should turn out ok. Or at least that is what I had been taught. But I was surrounded by, NOT OK. Bad things did happen to good people. No matter how much I loved those around me I could not protect them and keep them safe. No matter how loved I was or how surrounded I was with care, I couldn't shake the overall feeling of loneliness and despair. If, as I was taught, God was responsible, I couldn't figure out His motive or His plan. So, I formulated one of my own.

I decided that I was responsible. Early on I decided it was up to me to bring happiness into my family. I would dance around, make people laugh, distract them from the pain, not necessarily because I was happy, but because I truly felt that it was up to me to fix whatever was broken and I was to use whatever I had to do it. It is a crazy notion for a two-year old, but can you think back yourself and see where you, like me, took on the bigger problem because there didn't seem to be a viable solution available?

I think, to some degree, we all did it. I came into this

world and let's just face it, the world I came in to was broken. There was and still is an incredible tolerance on the earth for a truckload of crappy scenarios. Because I was given free choice, because the earth by its very nature is duality, I had come into an environment that bred both good and bad. Yes, I had this great loving family and yes, I was exposed to sexual abuse. Yes, I had a great dad who did so much for us but also one who drank because he had yet to discover his own worth and value. There was this balance between the two sides of the coin and I found that I was here to figure that balance out.

Don't get me wrong, I believed God was there all along, that a source higher than myself was available, but early on I did not see evidence by what was actually happening and what was being taught to me about what was happening. Where was this God? What was His job? It wasn't clear to me and I desperately wanted it to be clear. I knew even at two that this job I was taking on was impossible. As I grew older I knew I could not save my family and save myself. Saving my family required me to focus exclusively outside of myself and there was no way that path alone would or could ever lead me to discover myself.

So, I went looking for alternatives. I went looking for

meaning and truth and because meaning and truth seemed to be everywhere and within everything, I knew that it was necessary to take them and disperse them along my path, to take them both on the journey so that I could figure out how to love and honor my family, while also loving and honoring myself. I figured I could take these lessons I was learning, these pieces of the puzzle, and start to put them together in a way that afforded me a deeper understanding and knowing that my soul craved.

The scary part of this for me and probably for all of us is that to go looking for an answer to a question I formulated to make sense deep inside myself, it meant getting off the path I knew so well. And change really, quite simply, scared the crap out of me. At least I knew the predictable, at least I knew where the highway I was on was taking me, but the reason presented itself clearer and clearer, that to take that highway, to remain safe also meant choosing to continue dimming my light. And for me, I also felt that my actual survival was dependent on not dimming that light any longer.

I have this saying that I often say to friends and clients, that we are not here on this earth with seven billion other people to do this thing called life alone. We need others. We need other people to reflect back to us what we cannot see ourselves. We are all in this together. If I find my path, if I carve out a way that works for me, then we all benefit. But I couldn't start there. At the time, I couldn't make others be my motive. I had to start with me. I had to recognize the importance of others only after rightfully standing in my own spotlight. That was how I could address this alone thing. I could use what was already at my disposal, on my original path, but I could use it in a way that for me I had never seen done.

I have a sister, Rosemarie, who is five years older than me. In my early twenties, she often went to this woman who is a psychic and she would come back and tell me all about her experiences with her. I loved and respected my sister greatly, but I have to admit, based on my limited belief system at the time, I thought she was teetering on the edge. I listened and watched every time she came back from a reading, until my logic and reasoning path bumped up against my *"there may be another way"* path. It happened watching Rose. So, I myself went for a reading, actually over the years there were multiple reading I went to. This act of opening to myself in a new way, to a deeper voice, had opened a window, a possible way to look at my life differently. And a shift occurred in my aloneness.

I also needed more when it came to God. So, I

listened, I opened up, I prayed. I prayed to God but I decided to pray to a different God. I decided to believe that it was possible that the God I was raised with may have been short changed. That I may have been short changed. So, I watched and listened. And I saw that there may just be another way. I prayed and then worked to open myself to a different answer than the one I had always known. God began to speak to me, not from His high pedestal, but from a relational place, more like He was an old friend of mine and I heard His voice in a new way.

The trick here was not the psychic or God for that matter, the trick was within me all along. It was tapping into my own inner compass. My deep knowing that I did not want to be alone connecting with my deeper, in my core, belief that I was here to finally love myself. There were many areas in my life where I needed to redecorate. I had a warped idea about relationships, finances, work, play, you name it there was a distorted belief hanging out there. I also had distortions galore about my own worthiness.

But the funny thing about my compass is that when I finally surrendered to taking my less traveled path I realized my compass came equipped with intrinsic qualities that proved invaluable in every situation. It's like I was so terrified to get off the beaten path and then I was raped and it threw me onto a path I had never seen nor imagined. I had to figure out a whole new navigation system. In all honesty, this navigation system has taken me the last thirty years to formulate. It didn't come over night. I have read countless books, done therapy, meditated, done spiritual pilgrimages, and much more all with the desire to connect with and follow my own inner compass.

There is a lot of work needed just to undo the web of highways designed to keep us safe. But part of the recovery comes from realizing that the people who set up the original system were also flawed. Nobody ever developed an effective roadmap for "Others". These very people selling the maps had also been raised with distorted perceptions, distorted ideas of God and distorted belief systems themselves. I believe, at my core, that they were doing the best they could, but truthfully how good can the system be if it was developed by people who themselves felt alone and unworthy?

Waking up takes time, yes that is true, but waking up is the goal and deep in my soul I think I have always known this. If you are reading this book, you are on this journey. You are waking up. Any path will lead you home, that's true, but it has to be you doing the leading. For me to find a way out, for all of us to find a way out, we need to be willing to listen, not to that which is apart from who we are but to that which is deep in our core. And to find what is deep in my core? I need myself, I need others and I need God. With those three working together, the path starts to become much clearer.

I have never truly been alone, that is not possible but I did come to realize that the reason for so long that I did feel alone was because I failed to even take myself on my journey. Following that highway system set up with distortion after distortion was destined for failure because that system taught me to not trust myself and to leave myself behind. It taught me to trust the other and trusting the other has NEVER led anyone home. My path home materialized when I began turning toward myself, toward my own compass and realized that the journey could be fun if I actually came along for the ride.

STORY TWO – CHERISHED

Caring For My Mom

◆◆◆◆◆

The year is 1997 and I am living in Redmond, Washington. I have a good life there. I own a condo on the Sammamish River, I am working at a local community college and I have a solid group of friends whom I enjoy spending time with. Let's just say I have a pretty good life. At the time my mom lived in Spokane, Washington which was about 300 miles from me and unfortunately her health was declining.

My sister Rose and I lived close to each other and would often go together to see our mom. My mom lived alone. Mom was seventy-eight years old and was experiencing some health issues and was struggling with her self-care. My sister and I had tried numerous times to get our mom to move to Seattle but at her age she just didn't have it in her for such a drastic change. Because of this and because I knew something had to be done, I started entertaining the idea of moving back to Spokane.

I definitely had things to work through and process in order to come to a decision and to be ok with it. Spokane was where I had grown up and it held a lot of not so good memories for me. I loved my mom dearly, but it was going to take a major shift for me to make this kind of commitment. So basically, I went to work to clear the path to going back home and I told my mom that I hoped I would be coming her way soon.

Don't get me wrong, I loved my mom a lot and wanted to be there for her but I also had done enough work at this point to know I could no longer ignore my own needs for another, no matter who that other person was. And you know that alone feeling I described previously? Well even though I had grown and changed considerably over my life, going back to Spokane felt a bit like going back into the environment with which the alone feeling had been bred.

Since I was in therapy at the time and had a strong group of woman whom I was working with, I reached out and asked for help preparing for this next transition. I took a good six months to really figure out what my inner compass needed to keep me pointing in the direction of my own true north. In the end, I sold my condo, quit my job and said good-bye to my group and to my friends and I made the journey back to Spokane.

When I was growing up I probably would have just moved back and believed it was my responsibility to take care of my mother. But life is funny when you start to follow your own path. By following my own path, I got this wonderful thing called choice and choice proved powerful because it navigated through my life, not on some outward path, but through the roadway to my heart and toward my own unique inner journey. Choice spoke my language and it always had my best interest in mind.

Following our own path takes courage and it also takes curiosity. It's the "I wonder" mechanism of our life. I wonder what this next phase of my life will be like? I wonder how I can create an experience where my mom and myself can both get our needs met? I wonder how following my own path as it meanders back through Spokane can be a thing of grace rather than something to dread? And I wonder if I take this journey and I open myself to the wonder, how I can transform any feelings of aloneness and let myself truly feel and be cherished?

Cherished can be defined as to feel or show great love for someone or something and to remember or hold an idea or a belief in a deeply felt way. That, my friends, describes how I felt about my mom and how she felt about me. We flowed quickly into our grove. Mom loved having me home and loved the care that I was providing her. She immediately started taking better care of herself. We are beings of community. We are not meant to be alone. We each have so much to share but all too often our lives become smaller and more isolated as we age. This coming together offered both of us something. Coming together offered us both a way to see who we were through the eyes of love and to see ourselves reflected back from this love.

Being home became this wonderful classroom to do my work in. Caring for my mom became this exquisite opportunity to pull apart the threads of my aloneness and my unworthiness and to weave them into something that nourished and sustained me rather than something that tore me down. I decided that I was taking this opportunity to heal some of my old brokenness. I was taking this time, this cherished time, to reconstruct my emotions, thoughts, and ideas from this place of being cherished rather from the previous one of feeling alone.

This was a gift I was going to give myself. This was a gift I was going to wrap up for myself by creating new meaning and truth with my mom. I had a relationship with her up until now that had a lot of distortions and falsehoods scattered along the way. As a kid, I didn't always feel like I had choice but I could no longer say that. I did have choice now. I could choose to live in those old distortions and keep my life small and alone or I could challenge the distortions, get curious with them and bring wonder into the equation.

I was the youngest of my mom's nine children. Here was this woman who had nine children in ten years. She was a quiet and reserved woman. She had lost her own mother when she was six. She was a good mom and she took such good care of us but I can see now that she must have been so overwhelmed. Always having to be on, always having to provide care, growing up in a time where women were of service to others, not themselves. She did her best, I have no doubt, but her best was formed out of her own set of distortions she had been working from.

I, being the youngest, gleaned from my childhood my own set of distortions. I gathered together my ideas of myself, carved out of these distortions. Ideas such as I am alone, that there is not enough, that I am taking up space that others need, that in all this I have become broken and unfixable and unworthy. These may seem like strong ideas to form but I believe it happens to the best of us. We form stories in our minds from the experiences of our life, it's like a pre-paved path, but at some point, I decided I needed to rent an excavator and rip that road out. In reality, we all have roads that we need to rip out.

Like I said I had done a lot of work already on my path before I moved home to care for my mom but this became a time to put into action so much of what I had learned up until now. If I could go back into this environment where so much pain and anguish had resided, if I could go back carrying a different meaning and truth as my torch, what new discoveries would I see? What would be illuminated? What could I lay to rest and what could I discover and nourish?

We are powerful beings. ALL OF US!!! We each have an inner compass that if given time and attention will flourish. It will lead us home. Our compasses have always been set to point to our true north and our true north is our birthright but so often our compasses are buried under so much debris. Or we fail to see its importance because for so long we have been instructed to ignore it. My excavator was created out of my own questioning of these old beliefs and I used this precious time with my mom to dig out more of what was not true or relevant.

When I moved back home I was on this balance beam between my own needs and desires and my mom's needs and desires. If I wasn't going to embrace aloneness I needed to understand this dance from every angle. I needed to see myself as separate, as a unique being, but also see myself as a part of this bigger whole and to find the moves that would turn this into a dance of joy. Dancing with my mom was healing me because I was engaging in the dance instead of being a wall flower. My life on the sidelines was also a distortion I was letting go of.

I spent four and a half years with my mom. Because I was there with her and had opened myself to a new way, lots of good things came my way. Sometimes we would just sit together, share a game of cards, eat a good meal and watch *Walker Texas Ranger* on the television. It was a pretty simple life for my mom and for me. I being who I am talked to my mom about everything. My mom being who she was listened, took in what she could, maybe shut down a bit at my candidness, but always cherished who I was and was extremely thankful for this time we had together.

I was also thankful because taking this opportunity had opened a new world to me. I saw how much I needed people and how much people needed me. Not in a co-dependent way but in the way of cherishing what we have to offer each other. I saw myself as cherished and because I was cherished, aloneness and unworthiness no longer had such a place at my table. My mom's love, in the moment, showed me that love was possible, that there was enough, that I was enough and that I had always been enough.

If I had stayed in Redmond, if I had decided to not come home, if I had not engaged my group to help me figure this out in a way that would help me grow, what would have become of my life? Where would I be today? I can't really answer that and can't be sure of the alternate outcome but I do know that coming back home liberated me. It set me free. Coming home released me from so many distortions which allowed me to course correct and put my own compass in charge in a whole new way.

Throughout our lives, we have all experienced what we would consider good and bad situations. We have all felt alone and we have all felt cherished at one time or another. We have all most likely felt what it was like to put others needs in front of our own. And hopefully above all we have all felt the rush of putting ourselves first, if only for a moment. What is truly potent about all of this is finally getting that whatever the situation is, we ALWAYS have the power to transform it toward our highest good. When we trust ourselves, when we engage our compass; a powerful, magical lighting up of the field of life that is supporting us occurs, shifting the path we are on in ways we have only imagined up till now.

This life, right here right now, is what we have. Lots of water has gone under the bridge. Lots of stuff has happened; lots of ideas have been formed. As children, we really did the best with what we had and as adults we can go along and accept our fate or we can use each step along our unique path to transform what was into a life where we allow ourselves to feel and be cherished. We can lay to rest the old distortions, it is so possible, and in laying them to rest we begin to pave our own path to our exquisite self.

CHAPTER TWO

STORY THREE – DOUBT
Coping Can't Be All There Is

◆◆◆◆◆

Doubt has been a huge force in my life for as long as I can remember. Ever since I was little I have doubted if I really fit here on the earth. At the core of my being I felt like a mistake had happened and I had accidently been placed here in the wrong space and time. I just didn't feel like I fit in. I felt like a player sitting on the sidelines of life and had no idea how to get into the game. Being in the game seemed to be the point of life and yet I just felt ill equipped to do it with any amount of skill or proficiency.

Doubt is defined as being uncertain about something and believing that this something may not be true or may be unlikely. To doubt it is to not have confidence in it. I doubted myself. I was uncertain about so much. I lacked confidence in myself and I lacked confidence in this life and the circumstances that I had walked in on. I doubted my ability to do this thing called life. Really, I doubted just about everything.

I was born into a family that was struggling to make sense of it all and they had clearly already used all the physical, emotional and spiritual equity they had long before I appeared. This is not to say that they weren't rich in many ways, because they were, they were all truly beautiful people, but the system we came into was clearly broken and feeding nine new souls into this already bankrupt system didn't miraculously fix it. It just simply shined a light on the many gaps and holes already there.

There wasn't enough for who was already there and the scales had been tipped long before I arrived so I felt guilty coming in and drinking from a compromised cup. I loved these people, I didn't want to make it worse for them and taking where there was clearly none to be taken left me with considerable doubt. I was left with trying to figure out a way to cope with the immense burden this path had placed on my shoulders, a burden I could clearly see was also on their shoulders. Coming in on this road that said everything should be fine if I just followed it and complied. Everything should work out according to plan if I just listened and did what "they" said.

So, I followed, I listened, I stayed on the path laid out by others and I tried as hard as I could to be happy. But there is such a hopeless feeling that comes from trying to be something that you are not. There is an emptiness and we as humans will always look for ways to fill in the gaps to create some semblance of normalcy. We look for ways to cope because the doubt wants to eat us up.

In our world of duality, we can choose may ways to cope. We can be overachievers and strive for perfection, creating a façade that says we are thriving even when we are dying inside. Or we can be underachievers and get lost in the process of dimming our light and making ourselves small and insignificant. My family tended toward the latter. I think sometimes when there is an elephant or several elephants sitting right on your path and everyone is pretending they don't exist, well sometimes the goal becomes one of avoiding shining more light on the situation than is necessary.

So, with my doubt of myself and my light dimming presence, I coped by shutting off my light switch completely and making my needs nonexistent. I made myself small, I curled into a ball and I took up as little space as I could possibly do and still keep breathing.

I always wanted to believe in myself, I think deep down we all do, but the evidence that I gathered out of the crazy distortions that were my life, led me to this conclusion of doubt. There was really no other conclusion to find. To begin with I had already deemed myself responsible so this doubt was turned toward myself and toward my own worthiness. The very system I came into said if I did what I supposed to do, followed all the rules, kept my head down and stayed on THEIR road, everything would be fine. But it wasn't. What other conclusion was I to come too other than doubting myself?

When I started off life doubting myself so deeply and profoundly and found I had to keep moving forward and doing the next thing, I quickly learned that I was going to have to figure out a way to cope. The distortions just get to be too much and since as a child I often didn't have any control or choice on what was coming at me, I began to find ways that I could control and the ways I did find felt like I was taking some amount of choice or control back. Unfortunately, this choice and control came at a huge price.

As a kid coming into a family that followed the compass of the church and the compass of the community that we were living in, we were pretty much destined to fail. I mean it just can't go any other way. When the source of my power resided outside of myself, it just opened me up to so much pain because the other was never set up to be able to meet my needs. Hell, my family had a huge "V" on their foreheads. Victimization seemed to be our code. The "V" said victimize us because no one has our backs. Victimize us because no one is really watching out for us. As a child, I knew it was wrong not to love myself, God created me and He didn't make junk, but as far as I could see I could not see anyone living self-love as their truth.

I was the epitome of helpless. This is so hard to say out loud but it needs to be said and it needs to be heard. Not believing in myself, not seeing my inherent value, not sticking up for and embracing who I was and what I brought to the table only led to pain and misery. It only led to me being the victim because let's face it some humans, like animals, prey on those who are the weakest and most vulnerable. And when others preyed on me and tore me down the doubt and unworthiness provided the perfect breeding ground for more of the same.

For me, as I said before, I came into this life knowing that I ultimately wanted to love myself but there were so many messages that skewed how I saw myself. First, I grew up in a family that had a lot of brokenness. My dad was an alcoholic; I believe because he was forever putting the needs of everyone else ahead of his own. My mom had nine kids in ten years. She was known as a wife or our mother but she never really had any time or opportunity to be in the deeper part of her own being. They were both raised with so many distortions about their own worthiness, so many distortions about how they should live their lives, so of course doubt was a staple of their diet and therefore ours too.

And with that doubt also came ways to cope. My dad coped by giving until he bankrupted himself and then turning to drinking. My mom coped through doing for others, giving so much physically but shutting down emotionally to all of it. When it came to me I saw that the one thing I could control was what I ate, what I put into my own body, so food became my way of coping, my way of shadowing over the doubt and insecurities.

Counting on God to watch out for us was futile in my opinion because The God I knew of up till that point wasn't an open vessel of hope. He was stern and unforgiving and staunch in His belief that it was all up to me following someone else's path and plan. God did not have my back and I desperately needed someone to have my back.

So, what did I do? How did I survive and then eventually thrive? Well, life is an interesting case study. See I went along doubting and coping, coping and doubting but I got a bit older and began to see that there were other ways of going about things. My choice of horizons changed. Books have been a huge part of my recovery and awakening. I read books like, *You Can Heal Your Life*, by Louise Hay, and *Creative Visualization*, by Shakti Gawain.

I read those books till the covers fell away. And I read hundreds more because I realized I had a thirst inside of me that had to be quenched.

I went to see *Ram Dass* speak in person and then listened to his tape a thousand times. I took meditation and yoga classes because I knew I had to find a way to quiet myself and minimize the chatter that came from reading all the billboards and tuning into the messages scattered along my old path. I remember one time going to a workshop with *Geneen Roth* where she did this exercise where I told the voice inside of you to shut the @!&# up. That moment was pivotal to me because it allowed me to see that I was separate from it, that it wasn't actually a true part of me, it was just a voice and it could be silenced, it could be extinguished.

See the thing to know is that we are born into ourselves already complete. We have been and always will be enough in each moment, right here, right now. Nothing needs fixed except our belief that something needs fixed. I have a compass inside of me that knows my own exact coordinates, for Margaret Duffy, and I already have my path mapped out and it is one designed for ease and comfort not pain and doubt. But often times it doesn't even get a chance to pop up and be recognized because we turn our own channel down so low we can no longer hear it. But believe me when I say this, it is ALWAYS there and ALWAYS accessible.

Our true north is just that. It is OURS!! Our compass always points there but we have been brainwashed to believe that the answer is outside of ourselves. And it just isn't. This just isn't true. Everything we have ever needed has been right here all along. All each of us needs to do is turn our attention inward. We need to tune to our own radios and to our own channel. We should all want this for each other because we are all in this together.

Doubt can be transformed. We can turn towards ourselves and we don't have to continue to just cope. Not in the ways that have taken us all further away from who we really are. Turning in toward ourselves means loving ourselves as we are in this moment. It is realizing and then adapting to the notion that we are simply enough already. Doubt has no nourishment when we do this. We have no need to cope because our doubt transforms into wonder and wonder opens up a path of discovery that has always been there and is our birthright.

STORY FOUR – WONDER

Sisters, Sisters, Sisters

♦♦♦♦♦

When I was little I left my crayons out in the sun. When I realized it, they had already melted into little puddles. The colors had begun to run together and in doing so had formed new colors, brighter and more beautiful than I could have imagined. I hadn't expected these new colors. Seeing the crayons melted I had expected a mess but in the changing of form, the crayons turned into a surprise that seemed to hold endless possibility for something new.

Wonder is defined as something or someone that is very surprising, beautiful, and amazing. For me wonder describes my sisters. For me being the youngest of nine children I saw my sisters as those crayons. We were all individuals when we came together as a family, we all had our own spirit and our own story when we first met but in becoming a family, we became like the crayons melting together, creating a brand-new color combo. Wonder is present in life to balance the many facets of doubt that are also present for each of us. Wonder infuses us with an anti-venom so to speak. My sisters proved to be my wonder.

When we were kids, we used to watch *Irving Berlin's White Christmas* every year at Christmas time. There is a song in that movie that goes, "sisters, sisters, there were never such devoted sisters". My sisters and I would belt that out laughing and singing, it was like our signature tune. Being together often brought fits of laughter, the giggles, and downright hysteria. My mom used to get a bit peeved at us because she felt that our laughter bordered on being a little ridiculous. Maybe it was but it was also love and a deep connection that came from being together through the trials and tribulations of life while also having each other's back.

To be honest growing up we did not always see eye to eye. We struggled and fought at times. I know being the youngest I frequently drove my sisters crazy. I always wanted to be like them, around them and loved by them. That is just the way it is in a family. But it isn't all there is and it is so important to look at the total picture of your life not just the painful pieces. Choice has to be the driving force of life. Wonder is always present. Life can be so surprising, beautiful and amazing.

Life requires wonder. We need those surprising, beautiful and amazing things to help us make it through the muck. Just as in this book, there is a duality to life. Doubt is possible but so is wonder. Both are needed to grow and learn, both are present in multitude and both need to be understood and integrated into the whole so that we can move on our path toward home. You can't have one without the other so learning to glean everything you can from every aspect begins to weave our own beautiful personal soul design.

My oldest sister, Mary, was nine years older than me. As a kid, I so looked up to her and wanted to copy her ways and be grown up like her. I wanted her experiences as my own. My sister Rose was hip and cool. She was five years older than me and she just seemed to get "it". IT!!! And I wanted "it" so I wanted to be like her. And then there was my right arm, my sister Kathleen. Kathy was one year older than me and she was and still is my anchor. She was my partner in crime and I held a deep love and caring in my heart for her. Because there was our share of adversity present growing up, I needed to hold onto the wonder my sisters brought to the table. I needed to relish each moment and take in this strong medicine so that I could better weather the incoming storms.

My sisters were my fortitude. My sisters were my grace. Growing up I looked up to them and wanted to emulate them but as I grew and became an adult along with them a miraculous thing occurred. My sisters also became my friends. When I went to college in Cheney, Washington

I spent a considerable amount of time with my sister Mary who lived close by. We had such fun together. She had small children at the time so I got to spend time with her family and share in the new memories she was creating with them. I got to know her on a personal level and I got to receive back from her love and support. This helped to fortify me.

When I was in my early twenties my sister Rose and her two girls came to visit me when I was living in Tempe, Arizona. That was really the first time we spent time together as adults. We had such fun on that visit and we created a new level of wonder as we became friends. We began a lifetime friendship on that visit. We began to open our hearts to each other in a new way. We have had our ups and downs during our time together over the years but once you have someone in your heart they are there forever. Once you love someone and take them into your heart, really no one can ever take that wonder away or do anything to destroy it.

My sister Kathleen is the definition of wonder for me. I am still here on this earth to a great extent due to her. She has been my rock, my solidness and my anchor. She has cultivated such wonder for me that I look at her as a bit of a miracle in my life. She is grounded in who she is and what she believes and I believe she loves me unconditionally. That kind of wonder has needed to be taken in and infused into my being. I needed to use that wonder for my highest good.

Growing up the youngest of nine children by its very nature can present some difficulties. And having so many siblings it is only natural that we would fight and have our ups and downs with each other. When you have a house full of people looking out for everyone but themselves, you are bound to have issues that arise. You are bound to have conflicts, disagreements, competitions, and distortions. Don't get me wrong we had our fair share. But we also had a camaraderie that transcended all else. We may not have been super good at watching out for ourselves but we did watch out for each other.

We waded together through the trials and tribulations. We held hands with each other so that we didn't get lost. We watched out for each other when the coast wasn't clear and we formed a team dedicated to our making it out together and as whole as possible. We made each other laugh and feel joy and we had each other's back.

My sisters are one of the main reasons I am here today writing this book. Without ever saying it I knew I would be ok because of them. I knew I would be ok if I just didn't allow doubt to win and take me down. I would be ok with all the doubt that came with my life if I also could use this wonder to light the path out. The love of my sisters gave me this.

Today in every moment I need to recognize this good in my life. I need to drink it in. All of us need to take this kind of wonder in. It fortifies us. It is our shiny armor to withstand whatever comes our way. There is duality in life, two parts to everything on the earth. There is good and bad and for a long time I focused way too much of my attention on what wasn't working rather than on what was. And with this practice I received more doubt. Over time I have slowly learned that by focusing on the wonder present in every moment, the little pieces scattered along the way, I could begin to see the falsehood of my doubts. With this wonder there naturally came more worthiness.

If we can just be willing to turn toward it, turn toward that which can make us stronger, we can use it to build a solid foundation in life. If we do this, consistently strive for it, we will find that we are guaranteed a path richer than any we have ever previously imagined. This wonder, built on a solid surface, is there for all of us to venture out on to and it is a surface leading to self-love.

CHAPTER THREE

STORY FIVE – SORROW
My Brother's Four

♦♦♦♦♦

I was born into a family with five brothers. Michael, Patrick, Timothy, Kevin and Sean. It was definitely an experience growing up having five brothers. They were a crazy, fun and adventurous group of guys. They could be a bit overprotective toward their youngest sister who was venturing out into the world but their care came from a place of deep abiding love.

It was crazy having eight siblings all within ten years of each other. It was like there was a chain going between all of us linking us together. We had friends in common going up the line, we liked many of the same things and we shared thickly in the experiences of our childhood together. My brothers were definitely a different experience than my sisters were. They brought their own energy to the table. They had an energy, a vitality, a spark that was hard to understand but one that definitely drew me in.

They are included here under my story of sorrow because in my relatively short time on the earth this time around, I have lost four of my five brothers. This is a hard idea, even now, for me to comprehend. I have had my fair share of loss. Both of my parents are gone, all my grandparents and aunts and uncles. And several of my cousins. Really all the generations that came before me are gone, my siblings and I are the front line and our front line is dwindling. The loss of my four brothers, part of my front line, has been something beyond reason.

Sorrow is the distress caused by loss and disappointment and it shows up as grief, sadness or regret. Losing four of my brothers produced a lot of sorrow. It couldn't help but produce sorrow but if I allow myself to dig deeper into the story, if I uncover what lies below the surface, under the sorrow, then I see there is much more to the story. There is so much more for me to see.

Each one of their deaths caused a unique set of circumstances to play out in our family. In many ways, the first loss was the hardest because I was so young. My oldest brother, Mike, was only eighteen years old when he was killed in Vietnam. I was eight at the time. My parents knew it was a possibility since he was in the war but neither my parents nor I could ever have really prepared for such a thing so his loss caused a considerable blow to my family.

My mom collapsed into herself almost immediately, my dad hung in there as long as he could, caring for all of us but in the end, it proved too much for him also and he was engulfed in the grief and in the sorrow. Would you expect anything different? I think not, but for me, a little eight-year-old girl, I didn't have the tools to deal with such sorrow, this great loss which for me now didn't just include her brother, but also felt like I had lost my parents, caused a rift in the fabric of my being.

Sometimes this kind of sorrow causes everyone to fold into themselves. It is our protective mode. We didn't really talk about what had occurred and now what was occurring because of it. I really felt I had no one to talk to about it. It actually seemed selfish to have my own needs met. There was a huge elephant in the living room and let's face it folks, our living room was already teeming with elephants, so these elephants had plenty of company.

Sorrow expands and grows when it isn't addressed and my sorrow was reaching epic proportions. When I address my story of *Fear* coming up you will see some of the course I took and the consequences that occurred by this, "ignoring these elephants". The sorrow, dealt with so poorly in this instance, caused a major distortion to occur and littered my path with propaganda. If I was left with no tools, I guess I was going to have to learn how to improvise. For an eight-year old the options weren't many.

Now fast forward to my twenty-fourth year of life. I had learned a few things in the interim and they were about to be tested. I had moved home, from Mesa, Arizona about six months prior. During the move I had broken up with my boyfriend so I was definitely struggling a bit to find my equilibrium. Being home I got to spend a lot of time with my sister, Rose and my brother, Kevin. Obviously now we were adults we were sharing a newfound friendship with each other and we were creating new roles of being part of each other's support system.

During those six months, we went out a lot together and spent time evolving our friendship. We had great times together, laughing and crying. We shared some significant moments on our path together so when I woke up to the phone ringing and my brother's death on the other end, I have to say my world shook in a way it had never shook before. Losing Kevin was not as much about losing a brother as it was about losing a friend.

I have watched grief work its way through my family multiple times up till now but sorrow looked different this time around. We all came together on this one and we weren't hiding. Maybe I, maybe we, had learned something about this beast called sorrow. Maybe I was a little over ignoring the elephant because here I was together sharing in the sorrow of losing one so dear. And in sharing my sorrow, it began to transform.

We dug all our pictures out, reached into our memory banks and told story after story of our times together. Kevin was invited to the table, there was no covering up the loss, no hiding him over in the corner. We laughed hard as each story was told and we cried and cried and cried. We did it all out front and center. Sometimes someone would come into the mix who had just found out and they clearly struggled with our laughter and tears but if they stayed long enough the same circle that was enfolding us soon enfolded them.

Yes, I felt immense sorrow for losing someone I loved so dearly but we were also using that sorrow to warm us, to fortify us and to strengthen us. I knew I couldn't bring him back but I also knew deeply in my being that I didn't want to gloss Kevin's life over with his death. I wanted to celebrate him, we wanted to celebrate him, celebrate his influence on all our lives and to drink in the love and affection we had all shared so that it would permeate our very existence.

Opportunities arise every day in my life, in all our lives, where we are given a choice. There is always a choice. There were multiple paths laid out that I had taken before but those previous paths did not lead me to a good place. They didn't allow me to feel my sorrow, and to experience the depth of that sorrow and therefore they didn't lead me out of the sorrow either. Those paths kept me stuck in a distortion that catalyzed every step I took after that.

Losing Kevin became a choice for me to do everything differently. Just like the rape at nineteen, losing Kevin became a pivotal moment for me. He was twenty-eight years old and you can't tell me, I won't accept that these twenty-eight years was all the time he was given and that's it. No more living, no more chances, no more choices, just "it's time to meet your Maker". I just can't accept that. He had and he still has much more to do. And with this a door opened inside of me and some more of that wonder appeared.

The loss of my brother Sean came less than three short years ago. It was a different loss in many ways. For one I had warning. He was diagnosed with cancer and so I was aware that the clock was ticking. The grief, loss and regret were present but it seems that my brother had made a decision to use the sorrow steeped in his time left on earth to create transformation. He used the sorrow and his time here to make it into something much better.

The place where this unfolded the most for me was with his relationship with his daughter, Brittany. Sean held such a deep love for her throughout his lifetime but it was clear to me that he was going to capitalize on his time left to relish each and every minute he had left with her. There may have been an underlying sorrow there, it is understandable that there was sorrow there, but Sean had also devised a plan to change this, to transform the grief, loss and regret.

From grief sprung humor, lightheartedness, and hopefulness. Sean and Brittany loved their *Seahawks* and relished their time together cheering on their team. They laughed together and cheered together, sharing each special moment together. Sorrow could have engulfed them and could have buried them but neither of them would let that occur. They stood strong in their conviction and were content with this time they had together.

Instead of loss Sean was about having time, keeping his memories with Brittany alive and growing. He saw the gain in all of this, he saw the gain for Brittany and the gain for himself and he wanted to leave this as his legacy to her. He loved her so much that he wanted to give her gifts so that when he was gone she could take out her treasure chest anywhere she was on her path and she could see the beauty of their time together.

There was no regret. Instead there was delight and joy. Sean and Brittany took the time to relish and savor the time they had together. And in doing this opened up a whole new level to their relationship. For me it was a gift to watch. I believe it was a gift to all of us. It was a gift to see such a transformation of sorrow into a celebration of life and love.

My brother, Patrick, is added here after this chapter was finished. He just died last month. My brother struggled with his life. He never found a way to see past the pain of his life so he never found his path to the other side of it. He was pretty angry for most of his life and his anger shut the door on a lot of love and goodness waiting on the other side. When I went up to Washington for his service I went mostly to be there for my nieces, his daughters. You see every life, no matter how broken it appears, has gems. My brother's gems are his daughters.

My sorrow was different with my brother Pat. My sorrow went out to this beautiful human being who never actually saw his own light and therefore his own worthiness. He lived a life of struggle and there is more sorrow in that for me then in losing my other siblings. Ultimately all we will ever have, really have, is ourselves.

We come in alone and we leave alone but if we spend time in the middle getting to the message that we matter, that we are loved and that we are worthy of it all, then true sorrow never actually gets a foothold.

Choices, choices, choices. They are all around me, they are at every turn on this road I am on. Everything I encounter comes with a choice so I had better get busy choosing transformation over being stuck and over the distortion. Love can be found in sorrow and it is that love that transforms those deepest pains into deeper ah ha's. It is up to me, it is up to each of us and hopefully we can all see that being up for this challenge is so totally worth it.

STORY SIX – JOY

Lions, Tigers And Bears

◆◆◆◆◆

Since I was a kid I have always had animals. Dogs, cats, fish, rabbits, ducks, you name it and I have had it at one time or another. As a kid if one of my cats wasn't pregnant then someone in my family was bringing home a stray to add to our already large brood. Whether it was snuck in the back door or it was openly welcomed through the front, there was never a dull moment at my house. Animals were a big part of my life and the joy they brought to me was and is really undeniable.

Joy is the emotion of great delight or happiness caused by something exceptionally good or satisfying, it is pleasure and elation. Animals have so been that elation for me. Such delight in my life has been fostered in me through these unique animal relationships.

On the land where my house sat in Spokane there was a cottage attached to the garage. In the cottage, there stood an old claw-foot bathtub. My brother Kevin loved to capture snakes, turtles, frogs, fish, you name it he could catch it. There was a pond in the woods behind my house and my brothers were always bringing home their catch and keeping them in the mini pond we had created in this old bathtub in the cottage.

As a kid, I went swimming with my family in the Spokane River during the summer months and we always took our dog, Gus, along. The day wouldn't have been complete without him. Gus was a black lab with a family of nine children, so attention wasn't lost on him. He loved to do the things kids love to do and he showed it. If I needed a companion he was there for any adventure. Gus fit in so well because he loved mischief as much as I and my family did, yet he was so loveable that I couldn't begrudge him any opportunities.

To add to our animal adventures my aunt and uncle lived on a ranch one hundred miles from my house and we frequently visited on the weekends. I was lucky enough to get to chase chickens, cows and horses in my spare time. These animals provided me with the opportunity to expend all that pent-up city energy that had been stored all week. I could run and jump and laugh and play for endless hours.

For all that these animals offered me in play they also offered me so much more. They brought such joy into my life. Joy is a feeling of great happiness and these animals were a major source for this great happiness. They gave me such immense joy. I realized quite early in life that not only were they fun to play with but they were also very good listeners. Because I was the youngest of nine, having a free ear to hear my woes was almost unheard of. And being listened to, by the animals, was a joyful experience.

I remember early on talking to my pets about everything. I could tell them anything and they just went right along with it. They never questioned my reasoning, never gasped when I shared all the details, never thought what I said was crazy, or at least never voiced it, and they loved me, unconditionally. They loved me. They listened to my every word and they loved me.

I can't begin to tell you what a void that seemed to fill. In a world where attention sometimes was a rare commodity, their love was priceless. At the ranch, I would sit on a fence and tell the horses all about my despair. In the backyard with my bunny, Bowie Bowers, I'd cuddle with him often and he took in everything I told him and held it safely away. In bed at night my kitty, Tuffy, would sit at my feet and purr away, relishing the warmth and safety our friendship provided. They were my solace. They were my friends.

I don't know what it is like to grow up where there was someone always there to meet my needs. I loved my parents, cherished my brothers and sisters, yet I often felt lost and lonely so much of the time. If it weren't for my animals I don't know what I would have done. They gave me a voice, tenderness, love and acceptance. And they did all of this because they loved me and I loved them.

While at the ranch I especially bonded with the horses. The ranch in and of itself offered so much because it was a place away from my lonely life. The horses just added to the equation because they seemed to understand my pain and their presence simply absorbed it. I would go out to the corral and they would come up and lay their heads on my lap and just listen as I unraveled the twists and turns inside of me.

Growing up they really saved my life. They gave to me unconditionally what others put conditions on. The conditions were not always purposefully but when you are following a prescribed path, set up by strangers, it is often veering away from our deeper knowing about what we need and how to get it. I found that the animals naturally gave me the space to keep open and fresh to the possibility of love. Not romantic love but self-love. I learned of myself through them allowing me to be myself, to discover who I really was. They also taught me that for them, I was already enough.

Being out in the world can be scary at times. Sometimes it seems more like lions, tigers and bears, then kitties, puppies and ponies. I had come into this world with people who were struggling themselves, who were trying to figure it out as they went along, just like I was. My parents were often scared and confused and unsure of their own footing. My family was doing their best to navigate their own paths in life, while we were all struggling to make sense of the twists and turns along the path.

Life can be filled with distortions, especially since we often follow this predetermined path that, by its very nature, is filled with falsehoods. These falsehoods are present because the path doesn't take me or my individual needs into account at all yet strives to direct me on my way. That is a recipe for failure. I could not be given direction from a source completely separate from myself and neither could you. It simply never works out.

Most of the time I did the best that I could to just plug along. I don't think I consciously realized the influence my animals had on me until I left home for college. Once I had packed my car and made the journey to my new home the real impact became crystal clear. I actually thought I might die since I had not only left home but I had also left my incredible support system, my animal friends. This may sound like a strong statement but the truth was that all my true connections were so far away. I had friends now, was crazy about guys, had school and all the trappings yet I felt a bit lost not having that one being in my life that I could tell anything to and feel completely safe doing it.

As I grew older I got different animals along the way. Each had an impact on my life that was truly magical and far reaching. I think sometimes we need to take the lessons in any way they come to us. It's like we need to have a little scientist inside each of us and we need to learn to dissect our thoughts and feelings and pull out the significance of what we are experiencing. For me my animals were showing me my value before I could see it myself. They saw in me what I could not see in myself and with each encounter they were showing me more of my true self.

There came a time for me after the love of many animals where I began to make the connection with what it really felt like to be loved unconditionally. I think being loved unconditionally should be the most natural state that we ever live in but for many of us it isn't. We feel there are so many conditions on love, especially on the love we feel for ourselves. If we were only thinner, prettier, richer, more successful, whatever our poison may be, whatever is the condition we live by. Something is always blocking our joy.

The thing that I noticed though over time was how happy my animals were to see me no matter what condition

I was in. If I left the house for five minutes to get the mail, they were always waiting at the door for me, tails wagging. If I was sad they loved me, if I was happy they loved me, if I was angry they loved me. It never waned. No matter what was happening they seemed to love me and this infused me with joy. And with this joy came possibility.

I think if we look back we all have treasures stored in our treasure chest. Small happening that may not be significant to anyone else but have had a lasting impression for each of us. Once we experience joy, no one can take it away from us. It is stored there, deep inside, just waiting to bounce to the surface, ready to play again. That joy is just bursting with energy and it's wanting to reconnect to the depth of our being and to unleash its power on our lives. It is up to us to mine the treasure and to gather the jewels of joy along our path.

My animals brought joy into my life because they taught me how to love. They showed me what it felt like to be loved. I took that in. It produced joy and that joy fueled me to dig deeper, to grow my love, not only for others but also for myself, so that I could multiply my joy. And by multiplying my joy I was able to expand my love and therefore my joy beyond its original parameters to encompass people and things throughout my life. My joy began to permeate my life and that opened up a whole new path, a path paved out of the deepest most sacred part of me. On that path, I could not fail.

CHAPTER FOUR

STORY SEVEN – FEAR
What Is Really Eating Me

◆◆◆◆◆

So, speaking of elephants in the living room, my family had plenty. My dad's alcoholism was one of the elephants and it had a huge impact on my life. Well I should say that a bit differently. My dad's beliefs gleaned from the distortions in his life had a huge impact on me. His alcoholism was just the result from believing all the distortions. I watched my dad struggle so much of my life and all of his with these distortions and with the meaning he took from them. And it wasn't good!

My dad was a very selfless man and believed strongly in God, but one of the biggest distortions was doing this completely at the expense of himself. That never works. He always put everyone else in front of himself. That is what he had been taught. That is what he understood his faith said to him. And that is what I learned. Early on I got the message loud and clear and I put everyone in front of myself. I mean if you follow a path that others have made, how can you really ever listen to yourself and find your own voice? It just isn't possible.

[57]

If you are following this path and every direction you see steers you away from your own inner compass, at some point fear will become your guide and that is what happened to me. Fear is that distressing emotion aroused by impending danger, evil, and pain, whether the threat is real or imagined, the feeling of being afraid appears. Real or imagined, my fear became my guiding force. I didn't know another way. I watched my dad and my mom walk a path littered with messages of danger and experiences of pain. These messages were everywhere.

By the time, I came along my family was so entangled in the distortions that it seemed to be the norm and was therefore beyond question. We just did what everyone else was doing. We didn't question it, the very system demanded that we follow and accept it, there seemed to be no choice. It was the perfect breeding ground for fear and unfortunately when one lives so outside of their true calling, their true direction, they become so susceptible to the dangers of the world and therefore to the pain.

My life was no exception. I went along trying to cope as best I could. My dad's drinking just shook everything up and it invited in bad things. We were repeatedly victimized by beasts along our path and I couldn't stand up for myself, I had clearly gotten the message that I didn't really matter.

So, I internalized this great fear. I took it on and wore it like a badge of honor. But deep at the core of my being, deep at the spot where my compass lay hidden I knew something was terribly wrong and since I had no way to fix it I found a way to sidestep the fear.

We often want to have control somewhere, especially if there appears to be no control nowhere. We search for someplace we can put our mark, however distorted it is. I searched for that place and I found it in food. Food, to some degree, I could control. I could take it and hide it and get it out whenever I needed it. It changed how my body felt and I needed something I could control that would change how my body felt. So, food and I became friends. Food kept fear at bay. It nourished me in a way nothing else could.

When we are little there is really very little that we can actually control. If there is chaos in our life, there is also going to be fear. Some choose alcohol to cope with the fear, like my dad and as many other people in my life did, and some choose food. I chose food. I chose to numb the pain, to hide out behind the feeling of being full. I chose the feeling of having some degree of control over something. Food had taste, food had texture, food had smell, I could hold it and eat it, hear it crunch and I could see it just as I wanted to see it. I could take it in and somehow it overtook the fear and pain.

Food was something that awakened my senses. Fear had a way of dulling or even deadening my senses so having something that woke my senses up was very welcomed. Like I said deep inside of me was the true recognition of my senses but I didn't have access to that, at least not at this point, so I needed to find another way so food became my way.

But fear can't be tricked and food in my life was the trickster. See as I started to get older my emotion became much more complex and other things became much more important than the comfort that food brought me. Food brought me lots of comfort, maybe too much and with that comfort I gained weight. Gaining weight tipped the scales of comfort against me. I wanted to be loved and accepted but the signs along my path told me that love and acceptance were contingent on how I looked more than on who I was. Acceptance became tied to my weight so my comfort plummeted.

As I got older my emotions became so much more complex and they were woven into the entire fabric of my being, as was food, which meant I didn't have nor could I see a mechanism to separate myself from them. I ate to feel but the feeling became all twisted around this new view of being overweight and therefore more alone and undesirable. It's a rabbit hole we go down trying to find the exit out of this. My rabbit hole became to eat and then purge. I became bulimic.

I didn't plan it. I really didn't even know it was a thing at the time. What I truly think happened is that I ate to feel full, to feel whole, but then I purged because the emotions inside of me where so intense there was not enough room inside of me for the food and the new levels of fear. I purged because the pendulum had swung to the far left, I needed food to cope with the fear, but I also had new fears that made food the enemy. Can you see the lunacy in this? There is no way out. I was damned if I did and damned if I didn't. That equated to a lot more danger and fear.

Fear just doesn't let up and it becomes such an intense reality. It's like fear has a paint brush and it paints this immense picture in your mind of this terrible evil that is lurking out in the world and it whispers what is needed to keep that evil at bay. And you listen and follow the directions because with fear as your glasses it is very difficult to see anything else. So, I ate for comfort, tipped the scale too far and felt immense fear and then I purged to right the scale and bring myself back to equilibrium. It was a vicious cycle.

But the thing is sometimes fear gets tripped up by its own presence trying to be in so many places at once. See there does come a point where the pain pierces the veil, where an alarm goes off inside of us that we can't ignore. We bump up against it all the time and for a while we ignore it but there always comes a point that the pain of ignoring it is greater than the pain of denial. It is this point that we need to capitalize on. If we don't get it at first don't worry. It will eventually come back around. It did for me.

My fear pierced the veil I was hidden under when the pain of contorting into a smaller, lesser version of myself became too much. I looked in the mirror and talked to myself as if I were the lowest form on the earth. My expectation of myself was so far out of whack that it was impossible for me to be happy and like I said before, I desperately wanted to be happy. I wanted to love myself. Truthfully, I didn't consciously believe it was possible but there must have been a tiny light inside of me because I wanted to find another way.

This path we first get on tells us we need to do this thing alone. We can't depend on others, it's our responsibility to give but not to receive, that there's a limited amount in the universe and we are already at our max. But THIS IS A LIE!! The universe is abundant. Listen, there are not seven billion people of this earth for us to do it alone. I had to be willing to ask for help. I had to reach out and admit to someone else that I was lost and filled with fear. It was only by me doing this that I actually unleashed my hope.

See there are people out there that do love us, that do care, that understand our pain and also that know there is another way of doing all of it. When I kept to myself I felt fearful, alone and scared. But when I stood up and asked for help, when I opened my mouth and shared just a bit of the pain this amazing thing happened. In talking and sharing I purged some of my self-hate and this made room for something else to enter. I found another way to deal with my intense emotions.

Instead of hiding in my fear and eating and purging, I stood up and became among the counted. I shared my story a little at a time, let go of my fear and my aloneness and embraced community. Others cared and saw me and reflected back something I had failed to see before. There is something about acknowledging this wrong path we have been on and asking others to support us in finding our own path. Others can't find it for us, nor do we want to be invited on theirs, but they can show us that there is another way and love us toward finding our own way.

You see, loving ourselves is our true north. Loving ourselves is always what is at our core. It is the direction our compass is always facing and it is the only path that makes any sense. Your true north is yours, my true north is mine. There will come a time for all of us when we hit our bottom so to speak, scrap the bottom of the fear bucket and something strange and wondrous occurs. We turn around and look fear in the eyes and we say ENOUGH.

Sometimes it happens after a great tragedy and sometimes it just happens drop by drop through the experiences of our life. Sometimes it is an instant jolt and other times it is like dusting off an old book to see what was there all along. Fear has no hold on us if we face it. Facing it actually disarms fear. Fears power is in the unknown, fears power is in the falsehood of life but as we turn to face it, fear can't hold up the sham. Fear falls flat on its face when you look it in the eye because in truth fear is the coward.

Reaching out became my way. I saw myself reflected in so much of life and it was a good reflection. My path became this exquisite experience. I hushed the harsh inner voice and opened to a message that I had only dreamed of. I was enough, I wasn't intrinsically broken and my path was now supporting this knowing. It is uncomfortable to follow our path at first. Sometimes we even feel selfish, but that is just fear trying to reassert itself. The truth is that caring for ourselves is our greatest job and our greatest victory and caring for ourselves puts fear in its rightful place.

The elephant in the room is fear. Fear of exposure, fear of pain and anguish, and fear of experiencing much, much more loss. But facing the fear opens a window to possibilities beyond any we could have previously imagined. How different my life may have been at each turn had I not followed the prescribed path, nor ignored what was so blatantly obvious, but had courageously turned and looked the elephant directly in the eye and said hello.

STORY EIGHT – FAITH
The Person In Charge

◆◆◆◆◆

I have talked a lot about God so far. Being raised Catholic I started out with what I now consider to be a fairly skewed picture of life and of God in all His glory. The God I grew up with had a lot of rules and judgments that were fairly harsh and limited. This picture that was painted for me was tainted by people's deep fears and it just plainly limited God's magnificence. In the beginning scenario God and I weren't close. I was afraid of Him and I did not feel supported nor seen by Him. I felt very alone. He surely didn't have my back, feel compassion for my pain and quite frankly He didn't seem like one to be trusted.

Faith is a confidence or trust in a person or thing, often something higher than yourself. Faith is about having a belief, not based on proof, in another's ability, like a belief in God. Growing up the problem with faith is that I was supposed to automatically have it. I was taught to believe in something higher than myself but what it really came down to is that I couldn't wholly believe in something outside of myself before I first believed in something inside of myself.

The same psychic I went to in my twenties, told me her theory on God when I went to see her for my first reading. When she told me her take it rang so true it was like a huge alarm clock going off in my head. I will have to paraphrase it as it has been thirty years since that fateful day but it went something like this. She believed that we were created in God's image and that was what we were working back to be, like God. And because God was and is ALL things, we as humans live lifetime after lifetime coming back again and again to experience all the things that God already is, shaping us into beings of light and love.

As I see it in each life I am given an opportunity to experience through the eyes of each unique individual I become. I may choose struggle to learn or I may choose ease and happiness but each life is an opening to teach me. If I am someone who is persecuted, then I may in my next life come in as the persecutor. I may be poor, then privileged, uneducated then brilliant and alone and then surrounded by family. Every life takes place in this classroom called earth, allowing us to learn and grow as humans and as souls and to cultivate love.

With this perspective on God I now became part of the equation. It wasn't just me in a world of random happenings, but me in a world that had so much greater depth and meaning. Three hugely impactful experiences, the rape at nineteen, the loss of my brother Kevin when I was twenty-five and my struggle with bulimia, all catapulted me directly to challenge my faith because they shook my confidence and trust to the core. It was through these three things amongst others that I was able to come out to the other side.

Growing up with such a skewed view of God, I can now see why my view of myself was also so skewed. God and I were intrinsically woven together so if He was so mean and nasty how could I be good? If He was harsh and critical wouldn't the mean I would be too? The problem with that is that the harsh and critical me was turned in on myself and with that I became lost. There often seemed no way out of this maze.

My growing up had God judging everything. If I was poor, that was bad. If I was unsure, then I was weak. If I didn't give and give, then I was selfish. I couldn't win. No one I personally knew could win. Others seemed to win. People who had money, people who were beautiful or gifted or were possessing something other than what I possessed were often allowed admittance into the having academy. But I sat on the outside and wondered what I had done that was so bad that I couldn't go inside.

I think that this old God path is one of the harder ones to get off of when we start looking for our own way. For many people, I see them walking completely away from God because to follow any path toward Him seems restrictive and limited. But, for me I desperately wanted to find my own path toward a Higher Power that I believed would fill me up and make me whole. So, I set out on a journey away from this false God toward one of higher meaning and scope.

Maybe set out isn't exactly the right term. It may be that I was catapulted toward a different view of God. See tragedy often is the catalyst for change in our lives. When I was raped my faith was tested as much as it could ever be. If what I had been taught up till now was true, then how could this have possibly happened? I was a good person, I had followed the roads rules, and I had listened and conformed to the set codes in front of me. Yet here I was in pain like I had never experienced, doubting my very existence and questioning everything.

Every sign wanted me to hide what had happened, gloss over the effects, spin it in a way that made everyone else more comfortable, but being raped was personal. A generic road map was never going to describe a way out of this for me and believing in a God that didn't care was never going to help me heal. I had to look for a deeper truth and meaning because I knew at my core my very existence was dependent upon it.

Like I said before, what the rape did in my life more than anything was it caused me to question everything. This horrific thing made NO sense based on what I knew so far, so what I knew so far had to be wrong. Question marks appeared everywhere. I began to think that this path I was on may just be terribly wrong. My footing became so shaky and unstable.

When my brother Kevin died, I was again faced with questioning how it really was versus what I had been taught. My brother was twenty-eight when he was killed. He loved life but also struggled with it a lot. He was a good person but there was so much he still had to do and so much he still needed to figure out and learn. Being here for that short of time wasn't enough. This couldn't be it. There had to be more.

If what I knew of God was true Kevin was in for it and I knew at my very core that Kevin had so much more in store for him. He was just transitioning on so again what I knew of God had more transforming to do. I needed to believe in a God that had Kevin's best interest in mind. I needed to believe in a God that had my best interest in mind. I needed to open myself to a new path and a new way of looking at life.

With my bulimia, I saw that the power of this disease was dis-ease. I was not at ease with this path that I was on. I was not at ease following the rules of others. I was not at ease with having confidence and trust in everything outside of me, including God, and having no confidence or trust in myself. I was not at ease with believing that I was the victim in all of this and therefore I had no control.

I thought to myself if I have been created in God's image and that is what I am working back to be, as God is, then isn't my only real job to love myself and to treat my body as the temple it truly is? Isn't loving myself and caring for myself the greatest gift I can give back to the Creator and to the world? And if this is true then maybe God loves me unconditionally just like my animals, so maybe it is up to me to also love myself without conditions.

Maybe it's about loving myself regardless of what I eat or how much I weigh. Maybe it's about loving and nurturing myself through the continuous trauma of the rape instead of feeling broken and unfixable and therefore alone. Maybe it is also about staying connected with Kevin wherever he is and believing in his continued chances to strengthen his relationship with himself, with life and with love.

You know in my introduction I talked about my callings? Well I have known since I was a baby that my job this time around was to love myself. Don't ask me how but it has always been there. I didn't have a clue how to do it or even how to start but I wanted desperately to feel love for myself and to be ok with myself.

Because I started out on this road made out of distortions and pain it proved difficult to maneuver this landscape. The tools along my way, myself, others and God were dulled and frankly unusable. But faith is a belief not based on proof so it was up to me to turn this car around and find a way that would work for me. I needed to find a way that wasn't about beating myself up and was about cherishing what I was bringing on the ride.

Faith is confidence and trust in another but truthfully, I don't believe that is possible to have real faith in God until we have confidence and trust in ourselves. I believe we can only love and believe in something as much as we love and believe in ourselves. So, there is the work. There is the focus. God and the abundance of the universe, the field of life that is always there to support our every move, faith in this comes from connecting back to myself, back to my compass, and back to my core.

My relationship with God is only as good as my relationship is with myself. Confidence and trust in myself, in my path, in my ability to maneuver and to learn and grow, are the stepping stones to my relationship with God and my Faith in the goodness of everything. I can love myself easily if am following my own compass and heading toward my true north. If I can easily love myself then and only, then can I easily love God.

CHAPTER FIVE

STORY NINE – HATE
Giving Up On Self-Care

♦♦♦♦♦

It is hard to keep going sometimes. As humans, we are such creatures of habit and we often keep doing the very things that continue to throw us off. It can be so frustrating and confusing to try to figure out and understand how we can continue the actions that beat ourselves up when we so desperately want to change and do the opposite. We begin to hate who we are because try as we might we keep coming up against our old distortions and the limiting beliefs that spring from these distortions.

Hate is to dislike someone or something intensely or passionately and to feel extreme aversion for or extreme hostility for it, even to detest it. I know hate is a strong word but it does express how I have often felt about myself and about the circumstances within which I found myself. This hate often resided in a dark and deep place inside of me. I didn't necessarily want to hate myself or my path but when the gauge I had been given to measure my worth was completely outside of myself and was based on nothing I could control, I found myself predisposed to detest myself.

The gauge I was given was set up through a distorted lens. It was set up to generically track everyone and it gave everyone the same instructions. It didn't take into account any of my own individualism, or for that matter anyone else's. This made it a recipe for failure. I disliked myself intensely because when I saw the disparity between who I saw in the mirror and what I saw as the expectation for me I always seemed to come out on the short end of the stick.

It was torturous inside of me to want self-love and to want so much for myself and yet to be on a road that constantly told me I wasn't enough. Sign after sign on the road told me that I didn't matter enough to have anything that I wanted for myself. I wanted so much yet when someone outside of myself was giving me the prescription there was no way that the medicine was going to be any good for me.

The God I was raised with didn't necessarily hate me but I couldn't understand the rules of the road so I was constantly trying to shift gears to keep up with the constant expectations. I felt defeated much of the time and couldn't help but feel unsupported in every endeavor I encountered. My growing up God did seem a little vengeful and so did a lot of the people who were carrying His message. It felt so foreign to follow this path and yet it seemed the only way for a long time.

The people I encountered in my life often felt like they were against me, not for me. It is crazy how many distortions existed in the world and unfortunately still exist. Pick up a magazine, watch the daily news, look inside a newspaper or watch the television. We are bombarded with information that skews our view and does not paint anything close to the whole truth. We are taught things in school, by our parents, through family and friends and the church to look through a particular lens to see things and these things are simply not true. But what can we do about this? If it is all around us what do, we actually have control of?

Well the discovery that I made and continue to make is that I can control one thing in my life and that one thing is me! Maybe as a kid I did not have all the same choices but as an adult I do. I have choice. I have an independent mind and I alone have control over the thoughts that spring from that mind and therefore ultimately over my actions. I may have some work in front of me to take back my mind and the messages that spring forth from it but it is so possible.

For me the road back to myself had to involve self-care and it had to involve patience. I felt that I had fumbled the ball over and over again. I would try to put myself first and then fall flat on the ground. I knew what I so desperately wanted for myself and for my life but I often felt defeated by the old thoughts that told me to give up and to quit trying.

Patience had to become my best friend. I had to become willing to confront those old messages. I had to be steadfast in my resolve because I knew my compass had my best interest at heart and that the way out would require diligence on my part. See once that flash occurred that illuminated my landscape, I knew there was a way out. Now was the time for me to put my trust in my own compass, and it was time to align with my true north.

Changing the old messages isn't always a walk in the park. Sometimes it requires hard work and determination. I had collected an enormous stockpile of road signs that often detoured me from taking and staying on my new path. I wanted desperately to care for myself and to treat myself with the utmost respect but I was often derailed in my attempts and felt defeated once again. But patience lent a hand and pulled me through.

I asked for help from people who seemed to support this notion that my own voice mattered. There were books I read, seminars I attended, classes I took, shows I watched, and each one gave me a glimmer of hope that the hate I felt deep in my core could and would be transformed. Hate is a passionate feeling, an intense feeling and it can be harnessed for our own good and for our own unfoldment. Anytime we have such intensity of emotion we have a choice in the direction we want and need to channel it.

See this is what I am talking about when I refer to taking our own path. Good and bad aren't separate things if we are channeling them both toward our highest good. I did at one time have a considerable amount of hate for myself. I didn't measure up in any of the ways that I had been taught mattered. I didn't feel connected to myself and so I often did the opposite of self-care which lead to a much more destructive life. I turned in on myself and created an internal battle that never seemed to lead to a win.

When tragedy struck in my life I could have imploded. I could have been lost in that moment but instead I used the intensity of the emotions swirling inside of me to ignite the energy around the hate I felt, to ignite it toward my very own survival and ultimate thriving. It is like the flare of the emotion lit up every part of the road and when I looked around I saw that there was so much more to my picture than I had ever imagined.

See when somebody else is driving the bus we tend to

not pay as close of attention on where we are going but with every breath we can change this up. We can take the wheel and we can start driving the bus in the direction that fills us up. We have a choice. We always have a choice. Even when we feel like we don't, we do. It is really so simple. And don't get me wrong I know it can be challenging to walk to our own drum beat but we have to know and we have to shout it from the roof top, We Can Do It!! REALLY, we can!!!

We can turn that hate around, the intensity of it and the passion of it can be changed into something miraculous. That extreme aversion and that extreme hostility can be restructured. We have so much personal power when we plug into our own power source. Our true north is hard wired. Nothing that has come before us, no amount of abuse, no amount of self-loathing, really no amount of any kind of adversity can tarnish or damage our internal compass.

The mechanism that fuels and ignites our compass is ourselves. It is built in and it understands its job and it is dedicated in its one goal. Our own enlightening. No amount of hate can diminish it. We sometimes can bury it under the thoughts and rules of others but eventually we will simply hear our own voice piercing through helping us find our own path. We need to walk in our own shoes and when we do there in front of us in our path of origin.

And there is also self-love and self-care. See when you find your way back to yourself, hate simply doesn't have a place at the table any longer. Those destructive tendencies have less and less power. Having our first attention on our own needs and wants becomes the standard by which we live our lives. We erect our own road signs. We encourage those around us to do the same. We see the benefit for everyone in us focusing on our own map and therefore our own journey.

God and people take their rightful place along the road. Both add to the tapestry of our life but neither becomes so important or so significant that we abandon our own way. And our way isn't selfish or ego based. Our way is gentle and kind and loving because it honors spirit and earth. It honors everyone. It honors God. Self-responsibility heals all. Self-responsibility gives us back our rightful power. Self-responsibility and self-love heal the greatest rifts in the fabric of life.

Residing outside of myself created self-hate and loathing. It didn't contribute anything of value to the overall essence of my life because it took me so far away from the truth. And my truth and my truth alone is what was and is going to set me free. Just as yours will for you. If I could have one wish come true for this lifetime it would be that everyone's deepest desire was to love themselves too. To honor their own path and to forge through the mountain of self-hate to the beautiful landscape of self-love. That everyone would be the fullest expression of themselves in the world for all to see and with that the flame of all hate would be extinguished.

STORY TEN – LOVE

Life As A Tree

◆◆◆◆◆

So, I have a theory that I have formulated over time but that has come to a head for me now. While on this particular path I'm on I have come to see God very differently than I was first taught. Well actually it is probably more than a theory because a theory is a set of facts not known to be true or proven and I believe my very existence is proof of what I know. And what I know is that at the core of me, the core of all of us and the core of life, is *LOVE*.

Love is a profoundly tender, passionate affection for another person. Love is the feeling of strong or constant affection for a person. It is more than a romantic feeling or a sexual desire. Deep love has deep meaning. Love is the idea. The idea that we all came in, not to just find and cultivate love, but to simply be love, a deep abiding love that is saturated in every fiber of our being. Love is our heartbeat, love is our breath, we are love, and God is love. This is a very different scenario then the one painted out of hate.

I may be jumping ahead a bit here, going from hate straight to love but frankly it needs to be said. It needs to be shouted from the rooftops, "people, wake up, we are here to be loved, to be love". I believe it needs to be shouted because we have forgotten the most basic premise of life, we have forgotten why we are here and what our birthright is. We are here to love. We are here to be love. And we have always been loved!!

Trees for me are a symbol of our journey here on the earth. Wood is the primal material of the earth and of the universe. It is a very basic and powerful element, which is also exactly what love is. It is our most basic and powerful element and we need to see it, embrace it and cultivate it in our lives so that we can understand life through the context it is meant to be understood. Trees are an element that spring forth from the earth, reaching toward the heavens just as love does.

A tree grows from the earth. It is deeply rooted in the earth. It needs rich soil, rain and sunshine and with these, the tree grows up, up, up toward the sky. Trees branch out in all directions, growing and changing, always full of life. Trees go through cycles, at times losing all their leaves only to regenerate, sometimes flowering and blossoming with fruit and abundance. Trees are of the earth but also of the heavens. And so are we.

The way I see it is that our hearts were meant to be in

charge. Our hearts were the soul of our tree. Our mind was basically there to offer assistance. But a heart can't grow and expand and guide one that is lost on a road that is leading nowhere. Or at least leading us away from our core. Our minds took over for our hearts because the very system laid out for us to follow made it impossible for our hearts to stay engaged. It simply hurt too much.

See our birthright is a balanced system. We already contain within ourselves everything we need to be the highest expression of love. When we are in balance everything we need is there for us at all times. We won't want for anything because our first attention is on ourselves and on the field of life that supports our every move. This is our anchor. Our heart is our anchor. The rain and sun and soil are there perfectly balanced to allow us to anchor into the earth while also spreading our branches into the sky and living a life that bears much fruit.

Our birthright is a world of unconditional love and guidance. It is the principle that we are now and always have been unconditionally loved and guided. That we, at our core, have everything we need within us already to live a glorious life. That the universe is set up to support our every move and when we trust this deep guidance we will always be just fine. Love is that guiding post. If we love ourselves than everything is made possible through that.

We each have experiences throughout time where this love and guidance are our compass. Where we live our life from a deep place of knowing that we are enough, that God and the Universe are there to support and guide us, that there is so much abundance and that if we are in this place all is well in our world. Of course, what often happens, like with my life is that I learned about myself through a fairly distorted lens that guided me alright, but guided me with fear not unconditional love. Rebalancing this has become my work.

Life is about our taking in and receiving whatever we need along the way to live this unconditionally loved life. This act of loving ourselves and believing in ourselves defines the form that our experiences take. It is about being nurtured and cared for. When we are open and receptive to the abundance available to us our life works. There is much less expectation and much more flow. When we embrace this, we are balanced and our needs and desires get met through trusting that our unique path is unfolding under our highest care.

When I trusted everyone else's way my whole life was out of balance. Every experience I had was formed out of a distortion of that love and that trapped my energy and interrupted the natural flow. Then as I had new experiences, they were always based on the distortion and not the truth which further entrenched my experience of not being loved, deep to my core. Then I lived my life not from true love but out of the distortion of love. And life simply doesn't function well out of that distortion.

See I so desperately wanted to be love and to grow into this magnificent tree but I had forgotten long ago that it was my birthright to be unconditionally loved. I had forgotten that at my core, I was already everything I had been searching desperately for. I had, for so long, only identified with the distortions not with the truth. Even the nurturing piece threw me for a loop because I had always seen my role as the one to give love not the one to receive it. I was good at loving others; I was good at doing for others, but I was horrible at taking in that which was my birthright. And truthfully, I believed the distortion that I was unworthy of this love. I thought the goal all along was to look like every other tree in the forest.

I have continued to grow in this knowledge and have continued to deepen my understanding. I now see that I am unconditionally loved, I either remember this or I don't, I have the experiences of one that is loved, or I don't and from whichever belief I embrace, I develop my plan and live my life from a place of being in and of this love or I develop the plan outside of love, deep in the distortion. It is really pretty simple. I am always at a choice point. Love myself, don't love myself. Be happiness or be pain.

My internal compass is fully functional; it has just been buried deep under a pile of false beliefs. And it is up to me, it is up to each one of us to uncover our own pile and to change the story. If somebody tells you their way is the right way, the only way, run for the hills. If you pick a book up to read, know that you are looking for what speaks to you not necessarily what spoke to them. If you have a question, be willing to speak it out loud and if the answer doesn't seem to be readily available, stop, listen and be patient because the answer IS there. It is ALWAYS there. It has ALWAYS been there. And we are meant to hear it.

In this moment, what I have to be willing to do is to take responsibility for what I believe NOW. So as a kid I didn't believe I was unconditionally loved. I set out on this prescribed path and I took many turns. I formed ideas about myself that diminished my light. Ideas that came from people who had believed the distortions themselves. I felt alone and had huge doubts. I felt deep sorrows and with this sorrow formed deeper fears. And I had felt hate. But if I went back to examine my life I also had to see that I had been cherished and I had cherished others. I had experienced wonder and joy. I had developed a deep abiding faith and I had remembered love.

I have this saying I use often that goes like this. *It is not what happens to us that matters, it is what we do with what happens that truly matters.* So, we forgot we are love. So, we forgot we are loved. So, what!! Now is what counts. Now is the moment and I am shouting at the top of my lungs to myself and to everyone who will listen. I want to wake up but I also want all of you to wake up because I want this for you as much as I want it for me. I want us each to take the next step and the step after that on this new path, this path where the essence of everything is love.

I can just imagine a world if I were to wake up and feel love. Imagine if I were to look in the mirror and see love staring back at me. No more critical voice. What if I chose what to eat and how to move my body from a place of love? What if I met my family, my neighbors and my clients from a place of love? What if I felt it from myself, from others and from the universe and so did everyone else? Think about that for a second. Everything would change. Everything would expand. If I felt and lived unconditional love my experiences would change and from those experiences I would develop plans based on the truth so I would finally say good-bye to the distortions.

I can do this. I can uncover my true north. Love is my birthright. I can step up. I will step up, I will take radical responsibility for uncovering my compass and for realigning with the deepest part of who I am. I will ask for help; I will do it. I will reach out. I will look at all my experiences and I will find the love inside of each one and I will transform them. I will grow into the tree I am meant to be, reaching my roots deep into the earth and stretching my branches high up into the sky. And I will blossom from the nourishment of the love running through me.

CHAPTER SIX

STORY ELEVEN – DESPAIR
The Dangling Carrot

◆◆◆◆◆

All my life I have had this proverbial carrot dangling in front of me. You know the carrot, right? We all know the carrot. After fifty-four years here and countless encounters with other human beings, I think it is safe to say that the *CARROT* is very well known. The carrot was my direct link to despair. For me the carrot conversation went something like this. Everything would be fine if… I was only prettier, skinnier, richer, married, smarter and/or funnier just to name a few.

Despair was all about my loss of hope, my feelings of hopelessness, losing, giving up, and being without myself. This carrot apparatus came constructed out of despair on my predetermined path. I often felt hopeless striving for so much and obtaining so little. I felt such loss and wanted to give up because no matter how hard I wanted things and no matter how hard I tried, I felt like I was failing miserably.

Because I felt alone, because I had experienced such sorrow and because a lot of my life was riddled with fear my despair desperately worked its way to choke off any link I had to my happiness lifeline. Despair wanted to run the show and wanted to come in and illustrate for me why I no longer had any reason to hope or believe that my situation would improve or change. Despair was a powerful opponent. Despair was like a heavyweight fighter and despair wanted to win, to take me out of the game.

Because I had yet to really get and embrace my distinct calling, which again was deep in my core, that I was here to finally love myself, I had constructed this carrot as my beacon of hope. I truthfully thought that if I could just get these things I desperately wanted that I would be ok. If I was responsible for everyone else, then I was also responsible for getting the things I needed. And those things had to be outside of me because the despair continuously told me there was no one home at my core.

So, I went looking. It reminds me of the Dr. Seuss book, *Are you My Mother?* In the book the little bird falls out of its nest while its mother is out getting food and so the bird goes on this journey looking for its mother. It asks everything it encounters, "are you my mother?" The baby bird has never really seen itself so it doesn't really know what it is looking for. That was me. I had yet to look in a proper mirror at myself so I was going around, chasing that carrot, trying to find my mother so to speak.

I encountered many distortions though so finding what I needed and wanted proved to be a bit challenging. For one, no matter how hard I tried to get the carrot, well it just stayed the same two feet out in front of me. It was like running and running and getting nowhere. It seemed to me that the more I tried to catch the carrot, the more I felt like a failure. If say I lost weight, one of my constant carrots, and I achieved that goal I had been striving for but I didn't feel any different and it didn't really change anything then what was next?

Maybe I could meet the right guy? That always seemed to hold great promise. I would fall deeply in love, give my heart and soul to him, and then I would sit back and wait and wait and wait. What was I waiting for? To feel different, to feel ok and to not feel despair any longer. And because despair hung around and the carrot kept dangling there, I presumed that I must be faulty. It must be me that is broken and it must be me that needs fixed.

That is what despair wants you to believe. It wanted me to believe that I was intrinsically broken. That I was unworthy. That I was defective. Despair really gets its job. Despair is on to its purpose. But it is funny, this thing called purpose, because as I watched despair dig it's heals in, the Scorpio, Irish, youngest of nine, girl in me woke up a bit and started to remember her calling and her purpose. And she started to fight back. I figured that if I were eventually patient enough the pendulum would swing back. I just needed to be prepared when it did.

So, the pendulum swung by. It has had the tendency to do that over and over in my life and when mine did I realized that I needed to be ready to capitalize on it. I think what I began to get is that if I lived long enough, if I was willing to let people in and if I asked for help that these actions allowed me to begin receiving. So instead of always giving and feeling responsible for others, I was now ready to let something come in to me. And when receiving happened? Despair started to look a lot more like hope. Hope was hiding under there all along.

Life was always yearning to bring hope to me. Life wanted me to be well. The force and field of life always had my back and it always has. I am an absolute delight to the universe and because of this, life cares deeply about my well-being. This is the truth. The truth is that I am worthy, not that I am broken. The truth is that the universe was really created to support my every move, our every move, not to tear me or any of us down. It was created to support all of us. I have a choice in the direction I want to go, I have always had a choice and it was up to me to turn this vehicle around. It is really up to all of us.

See chasing that carrot was hopeless. The carrot was always going to be two feet in front of me no matter how fast I ran. It was always going to allude me. Being thinner or prettier or richer was not the answer. Anything I was looking at to fill me up that was outside of myself was never going to do the job. Because no matter where I go, there I am. If I am unhappy and unfulfilled no amount of cosmetic work will fix it.

So, I saw my work. I needed the tools to deconstruct this apparatus sticking out in front of me that was holding up my carrot. I needed to confront despair. I needed to call its bluff. And I needed to quit listening to everyone else's opinion and plans and to begin to listen to the small voice within me that was simply waiting there for me all along.

Sometimes when we have spent so much time outside of ourselves following a path built and landscaped by others we don't know how to reconnect. It may even be scary for us. I know it was for me. I almost felt like by opening this can of worms and by opening the floods gate I might drown. I actually wasn't really sure I believed I would survive. And truthfully this scared the crap out of me.

I think I also still held the belief that in order for true change to happen it had to be hard. This was a big one for me. I believed that change had to be painful to survive. With life, there was a price to pay. This message came from a place of not trusting myself or my own voice or trusting that the universe was actually supporting me all along. This has transformed for me over time and it is no longer something I believe but at the time it was strong and present. For me turning toward myself and really looking at myself for the first time required all the strength I had because it felt like I would be engulfed.

Feelings really want us to believe this. When feelings get disproportionately powerful, meaning they no longer do their original job, they lose all perspective. See fear is a naturally good thing, it keeps us safe, but when it gets out of control then it just keeps us small and insignificant. And in pain. And this is not safety. There does come a point though when the pendulum stops right in the middle. When this happens, it's called opportunity.

On one side is the carrot and our despair from yet another failure and on the other side is a thought. It is really quite simple at first. What I thought to myself is that I already felt shitty in about a thousand ways so if I turned toward myself could it really be any worse than it had been up till now? What I found is in that exact spot miracles occur. In that spot, everything changes. In that spot, I finally had my chance. And in that spot despair finally had a worthy opponent.

We come to this spot over and over in our lifetime. We come to this spot anytime we question a message, anytime we look in the mirror and feel love, when we ask for help, when we quiet our mind and listen and so many other times in our life when we stand between what has been and what can be. I realized that it was never going to make me happier to be thinner when thinner was the only thing that would ever make me feel worthy. Something else had to be my worthy.

I remember the first time I ever meditated. It was really quite funny in retrospect. Quieting my mind seemed nearly impossible. The messages were so loud and brutal. I had spent a lifetime looking to others for the answer. Praying to an unknown God for the answer. Looking up to people for the answer. Reading books for the answer. With meditating it was about quieting all of those answers. It was about making space for my compass to come into the light. It was putting all I knew, everything outside of myself, on hold. This was about dismantling the carrot.

Meditation was a direct link to myself. Instead of looking out two feet in front of me for the answer I was turning within. I wasn't rejecting everything I knew I was just making room for my deeper knowing to come to the party. Quieting myself let me hear myself. Not the critical, distorted part, but the loving, kind and caring part. And the part that was fine just as it was. There was no unworthiness there. There was no hopelessness. There was just love and acceptance and hope.

Meditation for me was a step I needed on the path to myself. I took this step because I knew I needed to quiet the voice. The voice was so strong and powerful and had become so distorted that it could no longer serve me. I knew that I needed to love myself and I knew that this old voice was never going to lead me toward self-love.

As with so much in my life I have learned that facing things is so preferable to ignoring them. Facing despair disarmed it just as facing my fears have strengthened my faith and dealing with my hate has grown the amount of love I have in my life. Facing despair, instead of drowning me, has given me more hope than I ever imagined possible.

Dismantling the carrot had to be done. Turning toward myself, which once felt impossible and scary at the beginning, has now become this playful, joyful exercise. Not having to live a life of hopelessness has opened so many windows and doors that the landscape of my life is forever changing, growing and expanding. The secret is that

I didn't give up. Through it all I stayed with myself each day as much as I could and each day that amount grew. There is really nothing better than that.

STORY TWELVE – HOPE
Margaret's Power

◆◆◆◆◆

We are currently embarking on a new frontier. Our ancestors before us were primarily focused on survival. They were following a path that was so entrenched that they didn't even question it. They were getting by and their roles were so clearly defined that there wasn't much room for interpretation. Our world today is very different. We have a multitude of choices for which direction we want to take and finally enough information has surfaced that we now know that our own way is there if we are only to listen.

For some time now I have been working on this idea of creating a relationship with myself different from anything I have ever seen or experienced. This kind of change doesn't happen overnight. It has to be shaped step after step. One foot in front of the other, walking, sometimes even crawling, along my path. At times, I have fallen back into my old ways, gotten on someone else's road, or read a sign and followed it even when I knew it wasn't going where I needed to go. Hope has always been my companion finding my way out of the storm and has frequently gotten me back on track.

Hope is that feeling that what is wanted can be had or the events will turn out for the best. Hope is to look forward to with desire and reasonable confidence, to believe and desire and trust. Hope in life is essential. I believe that even in my darkest times, if I were to dissect them, I would find hope nestled there. And because of this hope nestled there, I believed it was possible to find my way to loving myself.

At first, I didn't have a clue how to do it and when I looked around I didn't see a lot of evidence of people loving themselves in my life. Somewhere deep in my core the desire was just stronger than the doubt, to accomplish this task that seemed to be alluding so many. Sometimes we just have to trust that something better is there instead of what we can readily see. That is hope. What we want can happen. What we desire can come to be. Loving ourselves and living a life filled with this love and more can come to pass. The first step is just believing it is possible.

I really feel like I have always wanted to be one with myself. I have wanted to love who I am. I have wanted to cherish and care for and love myself as the most precious thing on this earth. I feel like I have been moving toward these new discoveries all the time but I also frequently have gotten caught in the loop where it always seems like there is one more thing to do to get to where I want to go. How do I move forward and manifest when these things keep coming up? These scattered pieces of myself that still seem to be out there and still seem to be broken. I know from fifty-four years of life that there is no there to get to so why did I sometimes feel a bit like I was on a treadmill where I felt like I was not really getting anywhere?

I felt like where I wanted to go was different than anywhere I had seen or heard of so how was I going to navigate an area so foreign to me? Along with this I had been looking at my relationship with God and had been wanting to take it to a new level of discovery. I so wanted to navigate away from the notion that there was one more thing to do or fix and then I would be ok. We are human beings living in a fractured world, if we look there is ALWAYS going to be one more thing. That is how it is all set up. The trick is not the one more thing, like I said before, the trick was and is what I do with that idea of one more thing. Do I load it up as ammo to be used against myself or do I take a closer look at it and see how it can possibly be transformed?

Hope is one of the tools I had at my disposal to bring about that transformation. But I had to decide if I was going to stay stuck on the old road, continuing to read and follow the old signs or if I was going to become a pioneer and embrace this new trail into my future. I knew all too well how to live in the old story and to make meaning out of the distortions. I had embraced that for way too long. I had lived my life in the unworthiness. I had let people victimize me and I had come to believe the story I had told myself for so long. But my compass was always there. The core of the truth was always there. Choice may have been buried but it was always there. When opportunity knocked, and opportunity always knocks, I had to decide to finally listen.

Hope sang a beautiful song when I finally stopped and listened. Hope belted out one hell of a tune. Hope filled the car radio with song and it was all about Margaret and her power. She was able to accomplish something and she was capable of so much. Driving two blocks out into my own future, I was going to experience a bounty because I was driving into possibility, not stepping back onto that predetermined path, created by others.

One of the ways I have kept hope alive is to continue to expand myself through my interactions with people and always finding ways to learn new things. There are so many pioneering people out in the world. So many people who want to expand themselves and also want to share their process to help others reach their true self. One such opportunity I found was a course called *Feminine Power*

Mastery put on by Claire Zammit and Katherine Woodward Thomas. This course was exactly that. Two women on their path sharing their experiences to help others transform.

This path continues to be monumental in expanding my own power. I have decided to take responsibility for my life. Responsibility for where I was, where I am and for where I want to go. For me this responsibility was plugged directly into hope because when I finally stepped up to the plate and took back control of my life I was immediately surrounded with hope. When I was blindly following the path laid out by others I couldn't help but feel helpless and hopeless. The very nature of following someone else's path is that I had to give up control. For so long I had followed a way that made me feel weak and broken down. Taking responsibility for my own choices and for where I decided to take myself finally put me in the driver's seat.

Being in the driver's seat empowered me because I could then begin to look at the distortions which were keeping me stuck in the old patterns. So much of my life had been directed from this broken place. So much of what I believed about myself, deep down, had not evolved. I was still carrying around a lot of baggage and in that baggage, were so many messages that made me feel increasingly helpless, and not hopeful at all. But my adult self was competent. My adult self was becoming responsible, my adult self was a pretty good navigator, and my adult self knew how to create my own map so that I could turn the corner onto my own path and my own way of doing things.

With the choices that turning the corner brought me, I could begin to really take an honest look at what was actually true for me and what was an old message. See the old path says it is the most important thing and the old path is completely outside of me. Getting on my own path put the spotlight on me. I was now the most important thing. That turn changed everything for me because feeling so responsible to others nearly killed me. Turning the corner toward myself was my salvation. I am not saying this was or is an easy task, but I am saying it is the single most important thing I have ever done.

I had looked forward to this change for so, so long. Remember, I wanted to love myself. I wanted desperately to be important to myself. If following that old path was the way to go, it would never have felt so burdensome and awkward. Hope was this tiny flame inside of me that kept flickering, trying to get my attention. Hope said to me that all that I had ever wanted could be had. It could be mine. And hope was right. Stepping into my own shoes has afforded me the chance to really be me. To take in everything that is true and real about me and to infuse it into my life. Hope has given me power and this has now changed how I see myself and how I show up every day on my own unique path.

CHAPTER SEVEN

STORY THIRTEEN – DEATH

Do I Stay Or Do I Go?

◆◆◆◆◆

Alone, cherished, doubt, wonder, sorrow, joy, fear, faith, hate, love, despair and hope. There is a whole menagerie of emotions coming at us along our paths. There is the yin and there is the yang. One side dark and negative and one side filled with light and optimism. Each step upon our path we have experience after experience that define our life and ultimately define who we are and who we become. These experiences and the beliefs formed from them can take us under and defeat us or they can lift us up and make us whole. The choice is ours.

Death is the act of dying, the end of life, the total and permanent cessation of all vital functions of an organism. Death is a part of life. No matter what is happening we are constantly up against the edge of death or the edge of life and up against the choices that ultimately make us burn out or come alive. Death can be our demise but it can also be our liberation. Death can be the doorway into self-discovery. Death of our distortions and the thoughts and beliefs formed out of those distortions can deliver us into a life with the power of a charging rhino.

We face death often on our journey. Literally and figuratively. We face it in our minds and through our thoughts. Death of the old and birth of the new. Death to the old ways of seeing ourselves, death to following this prescribed path and death to this trap that leads us into uncharted territories where the car radio is tuned to a channel we will never be able to hear or understand. It is funny because to stay on someone else's path is exactly what makes us feel dead inside. Trying so desperately to be something we were never meant to be causes us a lot of pain and this is so unnecessary.

For most of my life I have not wanted to be here. Early on looking at the meaning and truth along my path, I got the message loud and clear that I was broken and unfixable. Growing up the messages were so strong and they seemed to be coming from everywhere. Every sign I saw told me of the "right" way to go, what it would look like and feel like when I had arrived and what I would owe in tolls just for taking this road. With this I so often felt everything bad that happened was basically my fault and I was not empowered in any way to control it or fix it. I felt helpless, hopeless and defeated by this thing called life and I wanted out.

Because I had experienced so much loss in my lifetime and so much death early on, I used to just wish my life could simply be written up on a chalkboard and then it could just be erased. That way no one would be hurt if I were to leave and no one would even miss me because I would have failed to exist at all. I didn't want to commit suicide, but I hurt all the way to my core and if I could have just disappeared and stopped the pain, then I would have done that. Being on this foreign path was quite literally killing me.

Trying to live a life directed from some foreign source was going to get me every time. It just wasn't and isn't natural. For me so much of the pain I have experienced in my life has come from that fact that I myself have not shown up for myself. Because my locus of control was completely outside of myself, I wasn't allowed to come to my own rescue and quite frankly I had been dying because of that. No one else can truly know what I need nor can they meet all my needs, no one but myself. Yes, others can love us and guide us, but they need to love us and guide us toward listening, not ignoring. Ignoring and covering up my own voice caused me to want to stop being and to stop being only caused pain.

Being alive for fifty-four years and also having been a therapist for so many of those years, I have come to realize that this perspective of mine is in no way unique. Many people are lost and alone and are confused by the directions they have been given and many people feel the same loss of hope and the desperation of a life built on other people's meaning. And I think I know why. Being born and coming into my family and getting on this road set out for me, things were always destined to lead to failure. There is never going to be a good outcome for having all my attention on *OTHER* and on a road, that takes no account of my compass and therefore my own unique learning and my own unique soul and pathway.

There has never been a soul before me nor will there be a soul after me who is like me, I am unique. We are all unique and that uniqueness comes with its own spectacular road map. From the very beginning of life, we have been working back to this truth. No one outside of me can know or instruct me on my own way. My parents, my family, my teachers, society or even God and the church couldn't fully offer me access to my own map. They could offer guidance and they could encourage me to listen to my small voice within, but they were never supposed to take control of the steering and they were never supposed to control my every move.

Some might freak out that I include God on this list but I stand with that. If indeed I am created in God's image, then my inner GPS is already linked up and programmed to go in the right direction. My car, designed by God, came fully loaded. I can pray and ask God for guidance and I believe every time that God will whisper in my ear, "You've got this, look at your owner's manual, you are already fully equipped with everything you will ever need to make this journey". God designed me perfectly for my very own road map. I believe that God desperately wants me, wants all of us, to find our own unique way back to ourselves because in our creation, that way leads to our ultimate glory.

Getting on my own path led to the permanent cessation of the old way. Getting on my own path was the thing that finally swung the pendulum back to center for me. I had to come to a place where I was finally willing to lay to rest the myriad of distortions that were formed and multiplied through following someone else's way. Once I opened my ears and listened to my voice within, the path has continued to become clearer and clearer. Once I steered my way on to the path of my own making everything changed. I may have been scared, but I did it anyways.

See I came to a choice point in my life. If I was going to continue on I had to let the old way die. In my mind, I literally unzipped my old body, my old self, stepped out of the old suit and let it fall to the ground. I turned, said a prayer over her and then I turned again toward my new horizon. See, with the death of this old me such possibilities were born. I had chosen to stay and to fight for this life that sprang from my core. This incredibly life. I just didn't want to erase myself from existence any longer. Now I wanted to embrace who I was and embrace what I could bring to the world. My uniqueness could be the medicine that would ultimately heal me.

I have stepped up and stepped out every day looking at this new horizon and imagining what was coming next on the path. The longer I am on this path the less fear I feel of death. I have seen firsthand that death really only leads to some form of rebirth. Death isn't an ending; it is really just a beginning. Loving myself is really beyond anything I could have ever imagined. Loving myself has filled me in ways that when I started out, I could never have clearly seen, but that somewhere deep down I knew were possible. I just kept on my path and I kept listening. I asked for help from people in my life who honored my listening and who were also trying to listen for themselves.

Every moment is a new moment. If I get off track at any point I always have a new moment to course correct. Once I am on my path I am always on my path I just forget at times. Sometimes that old way wants to creep back in. At those times, I just need to stop the car, pull off to the side of the road and tune into my GPS. For me one way I do this is by just quieting myself so that I can really listen to what is going on. I may pray, take a walk, do some yoga, meditate or talk to a friend. There are so many ways and each time I stop to listen I build my strength and focus around this.

Each time I pull the car over and question an old belief I feel a release, a small death of the old and therefore a small rebirth of the new. And my horizon broadens. Embracing this path is what it is all about. Loving myself is what it is all about. The rest is mechanics. What I found is that the hardest part was uncovering the truth that had been hidden, but once I did that and choose life over death the road became clearer and clearer and therefore my way began to present itself differently in that very next moment. And I decided to stay and to fight for myself. I decided that being happy and alive was so possible if I was willing to come along on my own ride.

STORY FOURTEEN – LIFE
What Was! What Is! What Will be!

◆◆◆◆◆

Life!! There is so much to be said. I love life. I love this adventure that I am on. I love having this incredible opportunity to wake up every day and to begin anew. I love to live each day deepening my understanding of myself and of this gift of life I have been given. Of course, I have not always had this perspective, I have struggled in ways I would not wish on my greatest enemy but I have survived and conquered and therefore thrived. I have come out the other side of the tunnel and I am so much the better for it.

Life is that condition that distinguishes organisms from inanimate objects and dead organisms, being alive, reproducing, and having the power to adapt through all the experienced changes. I love that life, manifested by growth. What a beautiful concept. The power of adapting to our environment through changes occurring internally. Wow and YES!! Our internal changes that produce a life we can cherish and embrace have to do with finally uncovering our compass and turning toward our true north.

Our job here on earth is to wake up, to wake up to the true purpose for our life. Our job is to love ourselves no matter what. Alone, in doubt, in sorrow, in fear, in hate, in despair and even in death. To love ourselves while being cherished, in wonder, in joy, in faith, in love, in hope and in life. I speak a lot in this book about duality, yin and yang, the good and the bad but as I have awakened and embraced this thing called life through loving myself, I have come to realize that duality is really non-existent. Life is life, loving myself is loving myself. Yes, stuff happens all the time but since I quit taking and making personal meaning out of everything, I have been freed to just see what is happening as part of the process in this thing called life.

Since I have stopped hating myself for not living up to some ideal, I have gotten off the duality merry-go-round. I have stopped seeing everything that happens around me as further proof of my unworthiness. I have stopped taking every damn thing that happens personally. I have given up being responsible for everyone else and have finally just settled into the job of taking care of me. And the funniest thing has happened since I did this. The life that pulsates through me has stepped up and has taken up residency. I am finally my own driver, in my own car, with access to my own fuel and access to the best mechanic money can buy, me. And my engine purrs.

Pain is the natural by-product of driving someone else's car, on someone else's road, navigating to places we were never meant to be and reading signs that were never meant for us. Stuff still happens in my life, tragedies occur, people die, and things come to an end, but now I can simply feel the corresponding feelings without attaching unnecessary meaning to them. I can feel sorrow without attacking my own worthiness. I can face my fears naturally and see them as gifts that keep me safe, without having to shrink my life and beating myself up for the distortions that fear used to bring.

Stepping up and embracing my life has been a gift in so many ways. When I didn't show up to my own party, when I didn't even know I had my own car, I still desperately wanted to write. I am sure it was that still small voice within me seeking a way out, but for me writing without driving my own car made me way too vulnerable. See this book is me. This book is my story. And it is a direct link to so many distortions that it could give someone outside a way in. And that way in could be an opening to way too much pain. But loving myself and living in my own space, and following my own path, has built a fortress, a fortified place, a stronghold where I now live and breathe. I finally have figured out how to have my own back and therefore how to provide my own safety and security so with that the link in is broken.

Writing has been the very first thing in my life that I have done completely with first attention on myself. Writing, more than anything else, has shown me my way to myself and in that, the most natural way to God. Writing this book has been my liberation. Writing is me cruising down the highway in a convertible, wind blowing through my hair, the sun lightly touching my cheeks, with road signs that speak directly to me, seeing incredible scenery, and quite simply having the time of my life. And I could not have gotten here without the help of others. Opening my life to life has meant opening my life to myself, God and to the other beautiful people out there also finding their way to their own path.

One such person in my life is my coach and friend, Sara Dougherty, from *Passion4Possibilities Intuitive Coaching*. Working with Sara has been such a gift. For so much of my life I have put everyone in front of myself and I knew this was causing my writing to stall. I knew what the issue was, I had been working on it for long enough, but I also knew that trying to figure it out by myself was crazy. I mean there can't be seven billion people on the earth for us to do everything alone. Reaching out to Sara was about embracing my power not diminishing it. As with all things I have to continually question any belief that was formed out of the distortions and to challenge them as they rear their head.

During one of my sessions Sara lead me through a series of visions to help me get clearer on my path. Often in these visions I go to the places in the world that bring me the most peace. During one such session I ended up standing on the beach, on the edge of the water, staring out at the ocean. My toes were in the water lightly splashing the water and the sun was shining creating such a deep warmth. And here standing in the ocean I heard and saw a truth I had not seen up till then. I was the ocean. All the way to the horizon I was the ocean.

See I knew that in turning to my own path I had to embrace myself and therefore life but I did not really get until this moment how much I had believed that the ocean was everyone else and that they were all my responsibility. Even my writing was about being responsible to others. I thought I had to write, that it was my responsibility to others, and that I owed something to the world but this view sapped me of everything good inside of me. Standing on the edge of the ocean I finally saw that I had one responsibility and only one, and that was to myself. I always knew that God was there and others were there and I was there, I had just got the order completely confused.

In my vision, working with Sara, I finally saw that in order for anything and everything to work, in order for life to work, I had to rearrange the importance I gave to each of these aspects of life. Standing on the edge of the ocean I finally saw that I was the most important thing. I was the ocean all the way to the horizon. And when I looked at my ocean it was teeming with life. Whales were breaching, there was every color of fish, beautiful coral, waves crashing, and so much more. And in taking this all in, in seeing all this abundance I was finally able

to see God, I truly saw God for the first time. If I was created in God's image and I could finally see myself and finally see my incredible image, then I could also finally see God.

It was then in my vision that I looked up and down the coast and saw each and every one of the other, those I had spent so much time feeling responsible for, standing on the edge of their own ocean, viewing the magnificence of themselves. And it so clicked into place. They were all seeing their own ocean, themselves, and they were also then seeing God. I was a distant third and rightfully so. In order for me to write this book I had to get that straight. In order to write this book, I had to write it with my attention being fully on myself. I had to write it because every fiber of my being wanted to. I wanted to for no other reason than I wanted to for myself, to be the fullest expression of who I am. Writing is my vehicle. Writing in my life.

BRINGING IT ALL TOGETHER

◆◆◆◆◆

Let's face it. This thing called life definitely has its moments. Difficult, painful and sometimes disturbing moments. But it also has easy, joyful and wondrous moments. Each moment is exactly what is needed on our path. We may not want to face this or acknowledge this possibility mainly because if we take it on it is then up to us to choose the path and direction of our life. We will have to take responsibility and do something with everything we have been given.

I remember when I blindly followed the path others set out for me. There came moments when I would stop and just wonder what it meant to be on this path. For a long time, I thought it meant something bad about me, this path that had thus far been one of victimization and confusion. I didn't want to fess up to any responsibility for this mess. I wanted to blame others for my abuse and I often threw my hands up in the air because frankly it was so unfair and made no sense to me.

The truth is that life often doesn't make sense when we are viewing it through such a tiny lens. The victimization lens narrows everything you see and it ties your hands behind your back. If I was truly a victim in all these life circumstances that I have described, then frankly I was screwed. I could do nothing to stop the madness and nothing to stop the hurt and pain. If I had no choice in this, it only made sense that hopelessness would prevail.

I am thankful every day that this hopelessness option became completely unacceptable to me as time passed. Drop by drop the water of life smoothed the jaggedness of my beliefs. Sometimes the change was slow and steady, like in my relationships with my sisters, and at other times, like when I was raped, the jolt of change was intense. For me, both were needed. I had been hiding from the truth over and over till my fear of the truth just naturally became less and less and less. It's funny because the truth just is. The truth just hangs around waiting and being. For too long I played hide but not seek with it. But the truth is patient and steadfast. It just waits it out. It is always there, it is always visible and attainable. I just had to be willing to quit hiding and to turn toward it.

When I was, younger I had a lot of fear. I remember looking out of my peripheral vision and seeing mass blackness behind me and mass fear. For so long I was so afraid to turn and face that fear. I just knew that it would engulf me and take me into its folds. But I believe there comes a time for all of us when the pain of avoiding this fear is far greater than the pain of facing it and we finally find the courage to turn around. I found my courage and I did turn around to look fear in the eye.

When I turned around and faced my fears what I saw astounded me. Instead of an engulfing darkness there were just two floor to ceiling strips of blackness right where my peripheral vision had landed. Nowhere else. So, what appeared to me to be complete darkness, when I turned and looked at it, actually was just these strips, the rest of the field was light. All my life I had been sick with fear. Like if I turned around and opened this can of worms I would be crushed. I just knew it had its own strength and intensity. But the truth was so, so different. The truth was that there was much, much more light present then darkness.

All my life I thought I would get lost in it and never find my way out. And never did I imagine that there would be light along with the fear but there it was in all its glory. I could have kicked myself at this point. Why had I wasted so much time avoiding this fear? Truthfully, because at this point I didn't fully get it, I probably was too hard on myself but I did also cheer myself on for the courage it took to turn and face it. I cheered because I recognized right away that this meant something big for me. Putting the attention on me, maybe for the first time since I left source, was the most pivotal moment on my soul's journey up till that point.

Having first attention on anything outside of who we are is like walking around backwards. We truly can't see where we are going. We are bound to bump into things and fall. Life becomes slow and cumbersome. We have to continually trust the outside for information. We have to trust "the other", and let's face it they are not paying attention to what we are doing. Trusting others and not trusting ourselves is a one-way trip to misery. We trip over stuff, run into things, and basically become disoriented by always being blind to what we truly need and what we truly desire.

We are magnificent creatures, each of us, and God and the universe are just sitting there waiting for us to get it. They are waiting for us to see what has always been there with us, our complete selves. Every day I wake up I have a choice. Every moment of every day I have a choice. We all do. It is not always easy to choose ourselves, especially when the grooves in the road are so entrenched, but once I got over that initial bump, the road did get easier and easier. And it is not only that it got easier to find my own way, but driving myself generated its own momentum that helped me tackle each deep-rooted distortion that had plagued me for too long.

Every event on my path has helped to shape me. Getting lost and only following others has shaped who I am. Being loved and cherished has shaped me. Every moment of every day I have had experiences that have made me who I am today. When I didn't see the importance of myself and when I didn't see myself as part of the equation and as part of the team, I had a tendency to negatively take the experiences on as meaning something about my not being worthwhile. It was like driving a clunker and taking every shot on the road till my vehicle was almost un-drivable. Choosing to turn toward myself and to look at each event on my path in a new way has allowed me to change the meaning I had gleaned from them and has allowed me to heal and discover myself anew.

I often imagine what would happen if I were granted one wish. In my mind, there is only one wish I think of, only one wish I see as needed. If I got that wish I would wish for everyone to love themselves. Just sit for a minute and imagine our world filled with such love. Many may think this is idealistic, but I don't. I still have days when I doubt myself, days when I get sad or feel lonely. I still have days when I am scared to move forward and scared to become more of myself then I already am. But when I was younger and feeling lost, in my wildest dreams, I could never have imagined that feeling that comes over me now when I am truly ok with who I am.

Loving myself is a gift. Waking up each day and liking the person that I am is so worth it. Liking who I am in the world and being at peace with each step that has brought me here is beyond anything I could have imagined when I was lost. Being of service to myself is what allows me to be of service to God and to the world. Seeing every step on my path as a gift toward loving myself has freed me from the old story and the old meaning and that freedom has liberated me. I am now able to travel anywhere I like. The destinations are now endless with me in my life's driver's seat.

ONE LAST THING

If you enjoyed this book or found it useful, I'd be very grateful if you would post a short review on Amazon. Your support really does make a difference and I read all the reviews personally, so that I can get your feedback.

If you'd like to leave a review, then all you need to do is click the review link below for this book's page on Amazon here:

Amazon Review: Any Path Will Lead You Home

THANK YOU FOR YOUR SUPPORT!!!!!

www.ingramcontent.com/pod-product-compliance
Lightning Source LLC
Chambersburg PA
CBHW072026040426
42447CB00009B/1749